THE
UNITARIANS
A SHORT HISTORY

The
UNITARIANS
A Short History

Leonard Smith

Blackstone
Editions

Blackstone Editions, Providence, RI 02906
www.BlackstoneEditions.com
© 2006 by Leonard Smith
Second edition © 2008 by Leonard Smith
All rights reserved. Published 2008
Printed in the United States of America

ISBN 978-0-9816402-0-4

Front cover:
Michael Servetus, Faustus Socinus, Francis Dávid, William Ellery Channing; flaming chalice (created by Hans Deutsch for the Unitarian Service Committee, 1941); Joseph Priestley, Elizabeth Gaskell, Ralph Waldo Emerson, Bela Bartók
Back cover:
Hungarian Unitarian crest, flaming chalice (General Assembly of Unitarian and Free Christian Churches), red crayfish symbol of Raków, flaming chalice (Unitarian Universalist Association)

Contents

Contents

Part 3 - America

Part 4 - A Global Religion

Appendix

Illustrations

Foreword

by Charles A. Howe

This well-written book by Leonard Smith, though short, represents a much-needed, general, up to date history of the Unitarian movement. With newly expanded sections on Universalism and on Unitarianism as a worldwide religion, it covers the whole scope of the subject in a way not achieved since Earl Morse Wilbur's comprehensive two-volume history was completed in 1952.

The book is conveniently divided into four major parts, covering the development and spread of Unitarian thought: first in continental Europe, stemming from that of Michael Servetus, most notably in Poland and Transylvania; then its origins and development in Great Britain; followed by its evolution from congregationalism in America; and finally and briefly, its emergence in Africa and Asia.

The well-structured table of contents provides the reader with quick access to points of particular interest, the extensive bibliographic essay provides a guide to further reading, and the more than 60 illustrations help make the material come alive. Also included is a helpful glossary of historical and theological terms with which the reader may not be acquainted.

North American readers will find particularly helpful the section on British Unitarianism, drawing on Smith's background, including his tenure as principal of the Unitarian College Manchester from 1991 until 2002, a topic previously not well covered for the general reader. Likewise, British readers will find helpful the sections both on American Universalism and on Unitarian Universalism, the latter being the embodiment of American Unitarianism since 1961.

All in all, the book is an important and worthwhile contribution to the evolving history of the Unitarian movement.

Preface to the Second Edition

Nobody is more surprised than the author by the need to reprint this work only two years after it was first published. The intention was for the first edition to satisfy immediate requirements and remain available for about a decade.

The success of the publication in Great Britain led me to explore ways to make it available in the United States and Canada, and internationally, and I am obliged to Blackstone Editions for making it possible.

The new edition remains substantially as the first, with some corrections, modifications and additions. Chapters have been slightly reordered, US literary conventions adopted, and to make it a truly global study, a new section about both established and emergent Unitarianism in Africa and Asia has been added.

It is a pleasure to reiterate my thanks to all who assisted with the first edition, and for the first time to acknowledge fresh assistance from both past and new advisors. Dr. Phillip Hewett has not only clarified aspects of Polish history, but has kindly corrected the placing of the diacritical marks in the Polish names.

I am also obliged to Harris Manchester College, Oxford, for permission to reproduce its portrait of Robert Aspland, and to Dr. Roy Smith for the use of his photograph of Margaret Barr.

Charles Howe is the author of *For Faith and Freedom*, the most recent previous short history of Unitarianism, which makes his kind Foreword a particularly gracious gesture, for which I am most grateful.

My main thanks are for Lynn and Peter Hughes of Blackstone Editions, whose editorial skills have honed the first edition to produce what

I am sure will be recognized as an improved version. The revision of the chapter on American Universalism owes much to Peter and the new section on Africa and Asia is almost entirely the work of Lynn. It has been both stimulating and a real pleasure to engage with them, as fellow historians, in this project of transatlantic collaboration.

Leonard Smith
Arnside, 2008

Preface and Acknowledgments
to the First Edition

The purpose of this book is to provide for the general reader an easily accessible account of the emergence and progress of the Unitarian movement in its three major historic locations: Europe, Great Britain and America. There will however be some references to other areas and newly emergent groups, to extend the global perspective. The volume may also prove useful as a survey of Unitarian history for researchers studying its particular aspects.

When introducing his *Heads of English Unitarian History*, 1895, Alexander Gordon, the doyen of British historians of Unitarianism, described it as "an attempt to lay bare the framework of English Unitarianism, because it was less known than it ought to be" and because he believed that "the history of the Unitarian movement is the key to its meaning." In similar vein, this volume is offered with the same conviction.

It is not however written as a vehicle for propaganda, or only for committed Unitarians, but to provide a critical account for the benefit of anyone who finds the movement interesting and wants to know more about it.

Each part of the book can stand alone and readers are advised to select the sections that most appeal to them. Usually I have explained theological terms within the text, but a Glossary has also been provided to throw further light on aspects of history and theology that may be unfamiliar to the general reader.

Footnotes or endnotes, which might be distracting, have been omitted, but references are accounted for in an appended bibliographical essay, which also suggests further reading.

In most cases personal names have been anglicized. Hungarian names, where it is customary to place the patronymic first, have been reversed. For example, Dávid Ferenc appears as Francis Dávid. To identify Transylvanian towns and villages on modern maps, their Romanian names have also been included in parenthesis.

An inherent weakness of a study of this kind is that it can only be written from the perspective of its author, which in this case is British and more specifically English. Yet if this limitation is borne in mind, the work might provisionally prove useful in the motherlands of Unitarianism, and for those elsewhere who want to know how this liberal faith emerged.

The perspective has limited the title to *The Unitarians*, since Universalism, such an important feature in America, was only a relatively minor, if significant, phenomenon in Great Britain and is unknown by that name elsewhere in Europe. A description of Universalist origins is however included to explain Universalism's status in the merger of the two denominations, which took place in the United States in the late twentieth century, to create the Unitarian Universalists.

Many people have directly or indirectly contributed to the evolution of this book. In addition to my predecessors as principals of Unitarian College Manchester, who progressively developed courses that go back at least to Herbert McLachlan, and probably to Alexander Gordon, I am grateful to the distinguished historians whose works I have drawn upon and listed in the bibliographical essay.

The Rev. Andrew M. Hill of Edinburgh very kindly read a first draft and made valuable suggestions and corrections, and Mr. Alan Ruston, editor of *Transactions of the Unitarian Historical Society*, did the same as the work neared completion. The Rev. Sandor Kovacs, lecturer in Unitarian History at the United Protestant Theological Institute, Kolozsvar (Cluj Napoca), Romania, read and corrected the early chapters on Europe, and the Rev. Austin Fitzpatrick of Southampton the two final chapters of that section, from the point of view of someone who has had regular contact with Transylvania since 1989.

My wife Joan, and daughters and sons-in-law, Sue and John Dockrell and Gill and Col Reynolds, variously from Unitarian and non-Unitarian backgrounds, read the manuscript as general readers and adjustments were made considering their observations.

The Market Place Chapel Trustees, Kendal, gave a generous grant towards expenses. The crest is incorporated in the cover design by kind permission of the Bishop and Consistory of the Transylvanian Unitarian Church. The cover vignette of Elizabeth Gaskell is reproduced by courtesy of the University Librarian and Director, The John Rylands University Library, The University of Manchester; the Sozzini picture by courtesy of Harris Manchester College, Oxford, and the Priestley medallion by courtesy of The Unitarian College, Manchester. The Rev. Dr. Phillip Hewett kindly provided the picture of the parsonage at Raków.

Finally, while the work is an attempt to provide a global perspective of Unitarianism for an age that increasingly thinks and lives globally, it is equally to emphasize and value the particularities of its origins and development in different places.

Leonard Smith
Arnside, 2006

PART 1

EUROPE

1

Michael Servetus

A focus for the origins of Unitarianism in continental Europe can be found in the attack which Michael Servetus, the Spanish physician and theologian, made on the doctrine of the triune God in *De Trinitatis Erroribus* (*On the Errors of the Trinity*). It was published at Hagenau, near Strasburg, in 1531, only fourteen years after Martin Luther had begun the Protestant Reformation by nailing his ninety-five theses to the door of the Castle Church at Wittenberg, Germany, in 1517.

It has been suggested that the major reformers – Martin Luther, John Calvin, and Ulrich Zwingli, together with Erasmus, the sixteenth-century humanist – were not themselves at first greatly enamored with the doctrine. Calvin's theology in particular, with its emphasis on the majesty of God, left little place for the Person of Christ, and he himself had been under suspicion of being unsound on the doctrine earlier in his career at Geneva. Thus, when Servetus made his onslaught, at first rather crudely and later more moderately in his *Dialogorum de Trinitate* (*Dialogues on the Trinity*, 1532), it was necessary for them to assert their orthodoxy.

Servetus was not alone in the radical position he took concerning a range of doctrines which, when tested by the cardinal Reformation principle of the Bible as the sole rule of faith, began to look unscriptural and therefore questionable as a test of Christian faith. Across mainland Europe there were also other individuals and groups who, in espousing the new freedom, found that their theologies and religious observances were yet unsettled.

A primary concern was the question of baptism. Should it be of infants, or only of adults according to biblical precedent? Some, following the New Testament model in the second chapter of the Acts of the Apostles, thought the Christian religion now required a communitarian lifestyle.

Others renounced the use of weapons in favor of pacifism. A few, who also shared several of these other concerns, began to question the doctrine of the Trinity.

Early Stirrings of Anti-Trinitarianism

Early stirrings of anti-Trinitarianism arose in two locations, north and south of the Alps. To the north they were a feature of Anabaptism, while to the south they emerged among the new Protestant congregations in the Grisons of Switzerland and the Veneto district of northern Italy.

Michael Servetus
a seventeenth-century engraving indicating his ultimate fate

Anabaptists first appeared in strength at Zurich in 1525. Their name, meaning re-baptizers, was not chosen, but foisted upon them by detractors, as is frequently the case with radical sects. Virtually impossible to define because of its doctrinal diversity, the movement was nonetheless united in the common rejection of infant baptism as having no biblical justification. Instead, its adherents practiced adult believer's baptism, usually performed in the open air, in lakes and rivers. Other features of their lifestyle included socially radical experiments — with pacifism, communism, and millenarianism, a belief in the imminent establishment of a thousand-year period in which the Kingdom of God would flourish, either before or after the second coming of Christ — sometimes in ways that brought them into disrepute.

Savagely repressed, the Anabaptist movement was everywhere subjected to persecution. Great numbers of its adherents were slaughtered in Holland and Friesland. Their descendents became Mennonites, followers of Menno Simons, in Holland, and Baptists in Great Britain, Eastern Europe, and the United States. While generally orthodox in their beliefs, they also tended to question other doctrines on the same grounds as they had settled the question of baptism: that of biblical precedent. Some even went so far as to apply this critical test to the doctrine of the Trinity, failing to find any evidence of it in scripture.

As early as 1517, Martin Cellarius (Martin Borrhaus) denied that Jesus was God in his *Works of God*. John (Hans) Denck, a wandering preacher who found refuge in the relatively tolerant city of Basel and died there of the plague, was also anti-Trinitarian and unorthodox concerning the Atonement. In 1531, John Campanus was presenting Christianity in anti-Trinitarian terms in *Against the Whole World since the Time of the Apostles*. Others were David Joris, author of *The Wonderbook*, a fanatical character who eventually settled at Basel under the alias Jan van Brugge and lived a life of quiet respectability, only to be revealed as heretical three years after he died. His body was then exhumed and burned, and his family were required to do penance. More moderate were John Bunderlin, Christian Entfelder and Sebastian Franck, who were much admired as apostles of charity and tolerance.

These early radical reformers reflect the extreme theological and social ferment of the period, and the concern for new and revolutionary ideas. They are only tangentially related to later Unitarianism, as indeed they are also claimed as precursors of Baptist traditions. Many had little lasting influence, and the first major challenge to the doctrine of the Trinity came not from them, or indeed from amongst Protestants at all, but from within Catholicism, in the writings of Servetus.

The Reformation was essentially a phenomenon of northern Europe; south of the Alps it gained only a slender foothold in Switzerland and northern Italy. The powerful Republic of Venice rejected it in theory, though in practice it sought to avoid causing offense to German Protestants who came to the city or lived there for purposes of trade. The presence of émigrés from north of the Alps and the more tolerant attitudes this engendered led to the establishment of Protestant congregations in the Veneto, centered particularly on Vicenza and served by Anabaptist pastors influenced by Servetus.

Developments in the Veneto resulted in an Anabaptist conference being convened at Venice in 1550, to discuss the theme "Christ – God or Man?" Its outcome was an affirmation of faith declaring the humanity of Jesus. The meeting also appointed two preachers to spread the teaching, but one of them, Peter Manelfi, an ex-priest, later recanted and betrayed many to the Inquisition, with the result that the movement in the Veneto was subsequently scattered and obliterated.

Another important factor for the progress of anti-Trinitarian opinion in Italy and Switzerland was the influence of the intellectual circle of Juan de Valdés, the Spanish humanist. (Humanism in this period was not a theological position opposed to theism, as it is often understood today, but simply a scholarly tradition of devotion to studies that promoted human and literary culture.) This was primarily concerned with the reform and spiritual revival of Catholicism, but it nonetheless unwittingly paved the way for Protestant ideas through its emphasis on religious feeling, and its disregard for ecclesiastical authority. After the death of Valdés several of the group, including Bernardino Ochino, the leading Italian reformer, left the Catholic Church. Ochino fled to find refuge in London, where for a while he was associated with the Strangers' Church at Austin Friars.

A more immediate destination for those fleeing northern Italy was the relatively tolerant Swiss canton of the Grisons, where there were opportunities to minister to the new Reformed congregations. Camillo Renato, a Sicilian scholar active in Switzerland in 1545, was both anti-Trinitarian and critical of the doctrine of the Atonement. There were, however, limits to toleration in the Grisons, where the new ideas caused dissension amongst the churches, and the more radical leaders eventually had to move on to become disseminators of proto-Unitarian ideas elsewhere.

The Trial and Execution of Servetus

It was the writings of Michael Servetus, coupled with his martyrdom, which proved most significant for the emergence of Unitarianism in Europe and provide the main roots from which it grew, eventually to seed itself in organized communities, mainly in Eastern Europe where a climate of greater religious tolerance prevailed.

Servetus's need to operate undercover to avoid charges of heresy led to the adoption of aliases, including Michel de Villenueve, and the patronymic family name of Revés, which have resulted in the details of his life being fugitive and often conjectural. For example, his birthplace is not known with certainty. Scholarly opinion currently favors Villanueva de Sijena in northeastern Spain, though it was previously held to be Tudela in Navarre. His date of birth, given on the stone marking his place of execution at Geneva as 29 September 1511, is also unauthenticated.

It is not disputed that as a child he lived with his family at Villanueva, where his father was employed as a lawyer for the local monastery. The family were prosperous Catholics living in times of religious and political ferment, in a country until recently occupied by many Jews and Muslims. Spain had been at the interface of the Christian and Islamic worlds, and while there had been a measure of practical toleration, the Trinity was a particular cause of contention between the two faiths. It was a likely place in which there would be, on the one hand, controversy, and on the other, a quest for the doctrinal harmonization of views concerning the nature of God.

At the age of seventeen Servetus went for legal training at the University of Toulouse in France, where private study of the Bible led him to discover that the Trinity was not scriptural. After graduating he became secretary to Juan de Quintana, friar confessor to Emperor Charles V, whose coronation he attended at Bologna in 1530. He was appalled and disgusted by the papal pomp and luxury, and developed a profound antipathy to religious establishment.

Wishing to interest the Protestant reformers in his views, Servetus first visited Oecolampadius at Basel, where the impression he made was so unfortunate that the other major reformers were warned against him. An unsuccessful attempt to see Erasmus was followed by a visit to Strasburg to

DE TRINITA

TIS ERRORIBVS,

LIBER PRIMVS.

NSCRV=
tandis diui=
ne Triadis,
fanctis arce
nis, ab homi
ne exordien
dum eo du=
xi, quia ad
Verbi fpe=
culationem,
fine funda=
mento CHRISTI, *afcendentes, quàm plurimos*
cerno, qui parum aut nihil homini tribuunt, & ue=
rum CHRISTVM *obliuioni penitus tradunt:*
quibus ego ad memoriã, quis fit ille CHRISTVS,
reducere curabo. *Cæterum, quid, quantumq; fit*
CHRISTO *tribuendum, iudicabit ecclefia.*

Pronomine demonftrante hominem, quem hu=
manitatem appellant, concedam hæc tria. *Primo*
hic eft IESVS CHRISTVS. *Secundò, hic eft*
filius Dei. *Tertio, hic eft Deus.*

The first page of De Trinitatis Erroribus
(Hagenau, 1531)

meet Martin Bucer and Wolf-gang Capito. Obtaining no positive response, in 1531 he went ahead with the publication of *De Trinitatis Erroribus* and later supplemented it with a more moderate exposition in *Dialogorum de Trinitate.* The reaction was one of violent opposition from the major reformers. Servetus was forced to flee, virtually disappearing for twenty years.

The essence of Servetus's argument was that the doctrine of the Trinity is both unscriptural and unreasonable. He was hardly Unitarian in the modern sense, but approximately Sabellian, or a modalist. Sabellians took their name from the third-century Roman theologian Sabellius, who had held that the three persons of the Trinity are merely three different modes or aspects of the divine nature.

After the publication of *De Trinitatis Erroribus*, for which he used the name "Michael Servetus, also known as Revés, a Spaniard of Aragon," Servetus adopted the alias Michel de Villeneuve and went to study in Paris. Later he found work as an editor and proofreader at Lyons, where he prepared a new edition of Ptolemy's *Geography*. He then returned to Paris for the study of medicine. His treatise *On Syrups* was published in 1537.

His interest in theology appears to have been rekindled by his editorial duties on a new edition of a Latin Bible, which suggested to him the need for a radical, reformed Christianity. An attempt to interest John Calvin in his views led to a long and acrimonious correspondence.

In 1553 Servetus secretly and anonymously published his magnum opus, *Christianismi Restitutio* (*The Restoration of Christianity*), amplifying his earlier opinions. It was based on a manuscript he had already sent to Calvin, who identified its author, thus precipitating the final tragedy and martyrdom.

The *Christianismi Restitutio* was a plea for a return to a simple Christianity stripped of its accretions. Severely critical of the Catholic Church, it was also violent in its attack on the Reformers for not going far enough concerning the Trinity. The work also contained a denunciation of infant baptism and, by way of illustrating the Holy Spirit, the first description of the pulmonary circulation of the blood, anticipating by seventy-five years the attribution of the discovery to William Harvey in 1628.

Publication of the *Christianismi Restitutio* at Vienne in 1553 resulted in Servetus's betrayal when Calvin supplied the Inquisition with copies of the printed edition and manuscript. The book was immediately proscribed and all copies confiscated for burning. Only three are known to have survived: one at Paris, another at Vienna and a third in the library of the University of Edinburgh. Its author and printer were arrested on 4 April 1553. Servetus admitted his authorship, but disclaimed any intention of heresy. Realizing the danger, he contrived to escape, and the trial continued in his absence. He was found guilty on 17 June 1553 and burned in effigy.

Making his way to Italy through Switzerland, for some inexplicable reason Servetus called at Geneva. He arrived there on 13 August, intending to move on to Zurich the following day. It was a Sunday and he was obliged to attend church, where he was recognized and arrested. His trial continued on-and-off for two months. Calvin presented thirty-eight charges based on the *Christianismi Restitutio*. Servetus was found guilty of denying the Trinity and the validity of infant baptism, and sentenced to be burned at the stake, along with his book. The day after, 27 October 1553, at noon, he was led in procession to the place of execution, a hill at Champel, beyond the city wall of Geneva. As the faggots were lit he is said to have called upon "Jesus, Son of the Eternal God." "Jesus, Eternal Son of God," it has been said, might have been sufficient to save him.

2

Sebastian Castellio

The execution of Servetus had a different effect than the defenders of orthodoxy anticipated. It led to further doubts about the Trinity and a growing desire for toleration. Initial reaction was one of strong approval, with all the major reformers welcoming Servetus's liquidation. Among radicals, particularly at Basel, there were some reservations, and when, early in February 1554, Calvin issued his *Defensio Orthodoxae Fidei* (*Defense of the Orthodox Faith*), supporting the execution of heretics in general and Servetus in particular, there were further protests. Some were directly defensive of Servetus, others more generally of the principle of toleration. Of the latter, the most significant was *De Haereticis an sint persequendi* (*On Heretics, and whether they should be persecuted*). The work was published at Basel in 1554 under the name of Martin Bellius, which was later known to be a pseudonym for Sebastian Castellio.

Castellio was born in 1515 at Saint-Martin-du-Fresne, fifty-six kilometers west of Geneva. Educated at Lyons, he gained a reputation as a classical scholar, which in 1541 Calvin rewarded with an invitation to be rector of the college at Geneva. The friendship became strained, however, when Castellio became increasingly liberal and was denied ordination and entry to the city's company of ministers for his refusal to acknowledge the Song of Solomon as a sacred book worthy of inclusion in the canon. At a practical level his salary as rector was inadequate and he moved to Basel, where in the year of Servetus's death he became Professor of Greek. Eight years later, after the publication of *De haereticis*, he moved to Poland, where he died in 1563.

The major reformers were so alarmed by Castellio's plea for a more tolerant acceptance of heresy that a violent attack was made upon him in a letter sent by Theodore Beza to Henry Bullinger in September 1554. In turn, further defensive protests were sent to Geneva from radical reformers in northern Italy and the Grisons. That year, Castellio also issued his manuscript for *Contra libellum Calvini* (*Against Calvin's Book*), though it was not published until 1612. It was an eloquent plea for tolerance and humanity, which resulted in further interest in Servetus and a gradual dissemination of the principle of tolerance.

Sebastian Castellio
Professor of Greek literature in the University of Basel

The twofold consequences of the life and martyrdom of Servetus may be briefly summarized. His criticism of the Trinity led, first, to fresh views concerning God and Jesus, and second, to the adoption of new principles in the interpretation of scripture. If Servetus was the leading figure concerning the development of proto-Unitarian views of God and Jesus, Sebastian Castellio was equally important, if not more so, for the growth of the principles of toleration, which are fundamental to any understanding of modern Unitarianism.

Anti-Trinitarianism at Geneva after Servetus

After the execution, anti-Trinitarian tendencies continued chiefly, if somewhat ironically, at Geneva, among the Italian humanists who were members of a Protestant refugee community dating from 1542. Here the four leaders were Matthew Gribaldi, George Blandrata (Biandrata), John Paul Alciati and John Valentine Gentile. Gribaldi was only an occasional visitor at Geneva, whereas the other three were residents of the city and members of the Italian émigré church.

Gribaldi was a jurist, a native of Piedmont and professor of law at Padua, from where he fled the Inquisition in 1555. He was one of the first to condemn Servetus's execution, arguing that the death penalty was never justified for divergent religious opinion. Acquiring a copy of *On the Errors of the Trinity*, he quickly became a major exponent of Servetian theology. Later he was Professor of Law at Tübingen and a lecturer at Grenoble. Coerced into orthodoxy, he was nonetheless suspected of anti-Trinitarianism and as a consequence suffered harassment. He died of the plague in 1564.

Blandrata, who will be noted later for his influential role in Transylvania, was a controversial and enigmatic character. A member of a noble family at Saluzzo in Piedmont, he had studied and taught medicine at Montpellier and Pavia. As a leading medical expert of the period, he was subsequently court physician to the royal families of Poland and Transylvania. Converted to Protestantism by Camillo Renato, Blandrata fled the Grisons for Geneva in 1556, where he became an elder of the émigré church and its chief anti-Trinitarian advocate. However, owing to differences of opinion on points of doctrine, the church requested Calvin to draw up an orthodox confession of faith. Some members at first refused to sign it, but later all did so except Blandrata and Alciati. For them there was no other course than to leave Geneva. After visiting Gribaldi at Farges, Blandrata went to Zurich, and thence to Poland to resume a medical career.

Alciati, a soldier, was also from the Piedmontese nobility. After quitting Geneva he later joined Blandrata in Poland. He was also active in Moravia and Danzig, where he founded a small Prussian anti-Trinitarian group.

Gentile was one of the members of the Italian Church who at first refused to sign Calvin's confession, but later relented before subsequently readopting anti-Trinitarian views. In 1556 when tried for heresy and perjury, he was sentenced to death. A pardon was granted on condition of a humiliating penance, but he fled to Farges and Lyons, where he published his *Antidota* to Calvin. Further persecution caused him to seek refuge in Poland, but on his return to Switzerland in 1566 he was again condemned and beheaded.

The execution of Gentile evoked little protest. Anti-Trinitarianism was now effectively suppressed and all the Swiss churches officially affirmed orthodox belief. Nonetheless, liberal views persisted at Zurich and Basel, where the prominent figures were Bernardino Ochino and Laelius Socinus.

Ochino had been pastor of the émigré church at Geneva, where he impressed Calvin in spite of his friendship with Castellio. Later he ministered to the Italian congregation at Augsburg, but was forced to flee to London in 1547. He returned to Basel at the onset of renewed persecution under Catholic Queen Mary. It was from Basel that he was called in 1555 to be pastor at Zurich. Still regarded as orthodox, Ochino was banished by Zurich Council in 1563, allegedly for advocating polygamy in his *Dialogues*, a slur not uncommon against anti-Trinitarian radical reformers. As a consequence he went first to Nuremberg, thence to Poland, and finally to refuge with Anabaptists in Moravia. While not openly heretical, he has a significant place in the development of liberal religion.

Laelius Socinus was the other prominent figure to emerge at this time. Although later eclipsed by his more famous nephew Faustus, he has some claim to the title of "The Patriarch of Socinianism." Born in Siena of a family of patrician jurists, Laelius studied law before becoming interested in theology and a supporter of the Reformation. A friend of Calvin and Melanchthon, while he lived in Switzerland he became suspect for his alleged support for Servetus, though he protested his orthodoxy. When he died at Zurich in May 1562, his nephew Faustus Socinus, then at Lyons, inherited his papers. There is little doubt that these were an important factor in the later development of Socinianism under Faustus Socinus's towering leadership.

Zurich, Basel and Heidelberg

The importance of Zurich and particularly Basel as centers of liberalism should also be noted for the presence at one time or another of Erasmus, David Joris, Castellio, as well as Ochino. It was a refuge of freedom, if not openly heretical.

There were also sporadic outbursts of anti-Trinitarianism at Heidelberg, Germany, in 1570, led by Adam Neuser and supported by John

Sylvan, Jacob Suter and Matthew Vehe. Neuser sought the support of the Turkish Sultan, but when the authorities were alerted he escaped, leaving Sylvan, Suter and Vehe under arrest. Each was condemned to death. Suter and Vehe were reprieved, but Sylvan, despite recantation, was beheaded in December 1572. Vehe later went to Transylvania and became rector of the College at Kolozsvár. Neuser, now openly proto-Unitarian, also intended to go to Transylvania, but after many adventures and wanderings ended up as a convert to Islam in Constantinople, where legend has it that he experienced a grim and dissolute end.

As pioneers of a more radical and thoroughgoing reformation of Christianity than the major reformers were prepared to countenance, the foregoing would hardly have welcomed being so negatively described as anti-Trinitarians. Yet that is how history has come to know them, mainly at the hands of their detractors. In questioning the doctrine of the Trinity, the Person of Christ, and his Work in the nature of the Atonement, and because of the alternative views they were propagating, they might alternatively and more favorably be called proto-Unitarians.

However, at this stage they made very little headway. Indeed, anti-Trinitarian faith might well have died out, had it not been for two countries in Eastern Europe which permitted it to develop, on the one hand as Socinianism in Poland, and on the other as Unitarianism in Transylvania, a region now part of Romania, with historic, cultural and linguistic associations with Hungary.

3

The Polish Brethren

With anti-Trinitarianism effectively suppressed in northern and central Europe, it was only possible for it to develop into proto-Unitarianism in the relatively tolerant eastern European states of Poland and Transylvania, largely under the influence of refugees from Italy and Switzerland. Here it took two related, but distinct forms: in the Polish Minor Reformed Church (also known as the Polish Brethren) under Faustus Socinus's leadership, and in Transylvania under Francis Dávid.

The general cultural background of Poland is significant. In the sixteenth century it was a center of learning and enlightenment. Warsaw was a cosmopolitan city and Kraków had one of the oldest universities in Europe. The country was governed by an elective monarchy, and considerable power was in the hands of the nobility. Catholicism was not strong at this period and laws against Protestants were not enforced.

Reformation tendencies took root in several aspects: Anabaptist, Lutheran, Reformed and the Bohemian Brethren. The largest of these groups was the Reformed Church, supported by many of the nobility. By mid-century the country had more than two hundred Protestant congregations. Substantial numbers in both houses of the Diet were of the Reformed faith and the monarch, Sigismund Augustus II, though himself a Roman Catholic, refused to persecute Protestants. Moreover, the *Pax Dissidentum* of 1573 granted equal rights to people of all faiths, which subsequent monarchs were obliged to reaffirm.

Two major figures emerged as the early leaders of the Protestant faith in Poland: Francis Lismanino and John Laski (a Lasco). Laski was also influential at the Strangers' Church in London, where he was pastor during his exile. The first suggestion of anti-Trinitarianism in Poland arose, however, in a group of liberal Catholics at Kraków. An impression had been made upon them by an incident which occurred in 1546, when a Dutch traveler, "Spiritus," was glancing through the pages of their service book. Finding some of the prayers addressed to each of the three persons of the Trinity, he asked whether they had in fact three Gods.

Lismanino came under the influence of this group. Of Greek origin, he was born at Corfu in 1504, but brought to Kraków as a boy and then sent to Italy for his education, where he entered the Franciscan order. Becoming a protégé of Queen Bona, the Italian wife of King Sigismund of Poland, he went again to Italy. There he met Ochino and Laelius Socinus, and after studying Calvin became a Protestant. Returning home in 1556, he was responsible for the emergence of anti-Trinitarian tendencies within sections of the Reformed Church.

Peter Gonesius, who was born circa 1530 and studied for the priesthood at Padua in 1550, was also active in Poland. As a student of Gribaldi in Italy he was introduced to the views of Servetus. After visiting Moravia he returned to Poland in 1555 as a radical Protestant of the Anabaptist type, where Prince Nicholas Radziwiłł appointed him to a pastorate in Lithuania, then part of the Polish-Lithuanian Commonwealth. In 1558 at the Synod of Secemin he spoke of his Servetian convictions and thereafter, having declared his Anabaptist views, he went about girt with a wooden sword as a symbol of his pacifism. With the support of the Radziwiłłs, who provided a printing press, he became leader of a community of about twenty anti-Trinitarian churches centered at Węgrów.

Gonesius maintained that Scripture was the only necessary standard of faith; that God the Father was the only true God, Christ being subordinate to him; that the Trinity was a human invention not taught by Christ or the Apostles, and the source of all errors and divisions; that the Holy Spirit was not God; and that the only necessary sacrament was baptism by immersion.

Anti-Trinitarian tendencies also developed at Pinczów, where those who espoused them were designated Pinczovians. Nicholas Olesnicki established a Reformed church there in 1550. In 1557 Peter Statorius came from France to be rector of the gymnasium, where he introduced doubts concerning the Trinity, especially about the Holy Spirit. The situation was further complicated by the arrival of Laelius Socinus and George Blandrata, who in 1556 became a popular and influential elder leading the congregation steadily toward his own anti-Trinitarian position, despite challenges from the orthodox and warnings from Calvin.

Gregory Paulus, the minister at Kraków, emerged as the main exponent of Polish anti-Trinitarianism at this early stage. Tradition has it that while he was preaching against the doctrine of the Trinity from the pulpit of Holy Trinity church on Trinity Sunday, the building was struck by lightning. Those who saw this as evidence of divine disapproval were quick to set up an alternative Synod under the leadership of the ultra-orthodox Stanislas Sarnicki, which condemned the heresies of Servetus, Gribaldi, Gonesius, Gentile and Alciati.

Controversy was further heightened when Alciati and Gentile arrived in 1564, which was to prove a critical year. Blandrata was absent in Transylvania and Lismanino in exile in Königsburg. On the orthodox side Sarnicki called Christopher Tretius, an able Calvinist reformer, from Italy. In the hope of re-establishing some order, in August of that year the Catholic authorities issued the Edict of Parczów, which banished all foreign apostates from the Catholic faith, though later it was ruled to apply only to anti-Trinitarians. Alciati and Gentile were forced to leave, but Gregory Paulus, as a native Pole, was able to remain active at Kraków. As a result Sarnicki intensified his attacks on the "Arians," which in future became the standard designation for those who questioned the doctrine of the Trinity.

The Minor Reformed Church of Poland

It was at this point in the spring of 1565 that a group of nobles led by Jerome Filipowski, an anti-Trinitarian layperson, became alarmed by the Roman Catholic threat and sponsored a debate to coincide with the Diet of Piotrków. Intended to promote Protestant unity, it began in a civilized manner, but degenerated into acrimony and discord. Agreement could not be reached, and the result was the foundation of the Minor Reformed Church of Poland, the first organized anti-Trinitarian movement in the history of the Reformation.

Bitterly opposed by orthodox Protestants, the Minor Reformed Church sustained itself amidst a complex background of political factors, supported by the patronage of aristocratic magnates, particularly Prince

Nicholas Radziwiłł. It was formally established in June 1565 at the Synod of Brzeziny, which was much exercised with controversy on baptism, the person of Christ and radical social policies. Martin Czechowic and John Niemojewski, a layman and district judge, emerged as leaders of the Church's more radical congregations centered on Lublin. They rejected infant baptism and advocated strong social commitment, in which the churches at Poznań and Kraków later joined them.

The Minor Reformed Church was at first a loose and diverse association united only by doubts concerning the Trinity: the Son was not equal to the Father and the Holy Spirit not truly God. In 1567 the Synod of Skrzynno urged tolerance for the many differences of opinion concerning doctrine and practice. Some matters were to be left to conscience and the imposition of authority was ruled to be inappropriate in matters of faith. The parable of the wheat and tares growing together, only to be separated at the last, was frequently cited in support of tolerance.

Divisions concerning the Person of Christ fell broadly into four main groups. The Farnovians were upholders of a Christology approximately Arian. Arianism took its name from Arius, the Alexandrian theologian, who at the Council of Nicaea in 325AD had unsuccessfully argued against Athanasius, in the debate about Jesus's nature, that Christ was not eternal but created and, though divine, was subordinate to God the Father. It was when, after much vacillating, the emperor Constantine sided with Athanasius in the opposing view, that God existed as three coequal persons and one substance, that Trinitarian Christianity was established as the orthodoxy. Henceforth, Arianism was proscribed, though from time to time it resurfaced in various heretical movements down to the eighteenth century.

The Czechovians, followers of Martin Czechowic, asserted that Christ was a man, but rose to be God and worthy of worship; they were also opposed to infant baptism and were pacifists. The followers of Gregory Paulus were opposed to the adoration of Christ and committed to millenarian, radical social idealism and communism. Most advanced of all were the Budnyites, the followers of Simon Budny, for whom Christ was fully human and the worship of him idolatry.

An early attempt to achieve cohesion was a *Catechism* compiled by the moderate George Schomann, the minister at Kraków. It was the first statement of faith of the Polish anti-Trinitarians. The reaction to it

Simon Budny
Leader of one of the most radical groups
within the Minor Reformed Church

was renewed persecution by Roman Catholics and Calvinists. But the Minor Reformed Church nonetheless met with some success, particularly because of influential support and legal protection.

The monarch Sigismund Augustus was sympathetic and instructed his secretary to summarize the arguments for and against the Trinity, though the manuscript was suppressed and not published until twenty years later by the Minor Reformed Church's press at Raków. Also, after the death of Sigismund in 1572, all his successors were required to swear to preserve "peace among the sects."

Raków

Another factor for the progress of the Minor Reformed Church was the establishment in 1569 of a new "city" at Raków, funded by a Calvinist magnate Jan Siemieński, whose wife, Jadwiga Gnoińska, was Arian in her beliefs and a member of the Minor Church. Built fifty kilometers to the west of Sandomir, the town's name, meaning "crayfish," was taken from the armorial bearings of the Gnoiński family. For fifty years Raków was the great center of Polish anti-Trinitarianism. From its academy scholarly ministers traveled to propagate Socinian ideas across Europe, supported by a prodigious literature issuing from its press.

Arms of the Gnoińsky family
Raków took its name from the rak *(crayfish).*

Doctrinal and social controversies nonetheless remained unsettled. The Minor Reformed Church lacked effective leadership until the arrival of Faustus Socinus from Transylvania in 1580. Gradually, by patient persuasion, Socinus organized the Church into a consistent system, avoiding extremes and ably representing the movement in disputes with Roman Catholics and orthodox Protestants. Indeed, so important was his influence that the movement eventually came to be called "Socinian." Socinus and the members of the Minor Reformed Church never actually used the term themselves, preferring to be known as mere Christians, Catholic Christians, or more commonly the Polish Brethren.

4

Faustus Socinus

After its separation from the Reformed Church in 1565, the Polish anti-Trinitarian Minor Reformed Church was for a few years riven by internal disputes. Moreover, externally the national crisis of 1572-1575 raised the question of the use of arms, dividing the pacifist communitarians of Raków against the Budnyites outside the settlement.

In looking to Socinus for leadership to resolve their differences, the Racovians could expect him to support their pacifism, while the Budnyites knew he was not committed to the necessity of adult re-baptism, which the Racovians required. Of his arrival from Transylvania in 1580, his grandson, Andrew Wiszowaty, recorded that he was refused admission to the Minor Church for "disagreeing on certain doctrines; nor was he admitted to the holy Supper; yet in defense of these churches he contended actively in his writings against their antagonists."

Socinus is arguably the second most important name after Servetus in any consideration of European Unitarian origins, particularly as the role of Francis Dávid is more confined to Transylvania. Born at Siena, he was the nephew of Laelius Socinus and a member of a family of patrician lawyers extending over several generations. The Sozzini had a palazzo in the city and a villa at Scopeto, eight kilometers to the northeast, which became a meeting-place for humanists, artists and writers, and a refuge for religious dissidents. The estate ceased to be owned by the Sozzini in mid-nineteenth century, but it survives today as Borgo Scopeto, producing a fine Chianti Classico.

After his father's death, when he was only two years old, the family went into exile at Lyons, from where Socinus visited Geneva and had contact with the Italian refugees.

Faustus Socinus

On the death of Laelius at Zurich in May 1562, Faustus took charge of his uncle's papers. He was not noticeably radical at this stage, and between 1563 and 1575 he was a courtier in the service of Isabella de Medici at Florence, where he published *De Sacrae Scripturae Auctoritate* (*On the Authority of Scripture*). On Isabella's death he moved to Basel, where in 1578 he wrote *De Jesu Christo servatore* (*On Christ the Savior*), which was published in 1594. In this work he uses the term "servator" rather than "salvator" and argues his view of the doctrine of the Atonement: that Christ is savior not because he suffered for humanity's sins, or died to appease God's wrath, but because he died as a servant showing the way to Eternal Life. Salvation comes through following him. It was not dissimilar to the view held in the twelfth century by Peter Abelard.

An invitation to Socinus to come to Poland was first issued by George Blandrata, who wanted him to support his own contention that worship should be offered to Christ. It was this adorantist view that eventually became the main cause of disagreement between the Socinians and the Unitarian followers of Francis Dávid in Transylvania, who regarded the adoration of Christ as idolatry. In the event he was to remain in Poland for twenty-four years.

Socinus was first associated with an Anabaptist group at Kraków. His influence was increased by marriage in 1586 to Elizabeth Morsztyn, a Polish nobleman's daughter, who died a year later shortly after the birth of their daughter Agnes. At synods in 1584 he was arguing against the immediate Second Coming and in favor of the worship of Christ. By 1588 he was the accepted leader of the Minor Reformed Church, though he was never a formal member, nor ever a resident of Raków.

In 1587 the Inquisition confiscated Socinus's property in Italy, while in Poland he was increasingly the object of anti-Protestant campaigns engineered by the Jesuits, particularly after the publication of *On Christ the Savior* in 1594. A victim of two mob assaults, in 1598 he only escaped through the intervention of the rector and one of the professors of Kraków University.

Seeking a quieter sphere, Socinus moved to the village of Lucławice, where until his death he enjoyed the friendship and protection of the local landowner and the Minor Reformed Church minister, Peter Statorius, Jr. In 1601/2 he supervised two theological seminars reviewing all aspects of Christian thought and practice, championing a moderate, progressive, rational approach, in opposition to the more literal and conservative Czechowic. He also began to collect and revise his writings ready for publication or reprinting and, assisted by the scholarly Statorius, he returned to a long-standing project, the publication of a fully revised Catechism. The completion of the work was, however, forestalled by his death on 3 March 1604 and that of Statorius the following year.

The Minor Reformed Church then made great efforts to collect and preserve his writings. During the next twenty-five years there was a steady stream of publications, including German and Dutch translations. Circulated throughout Europe, these had considerable influence in the spread of Socinian doctrine. The complete works were eventually published at Amsterdam as the *Bibliotheca Fratrum Polonorum* (*The Library of the Polish Brethren*).

The Racovian Catechism

The *Racovian Catechism* of 1605 was the realization of Socinus's last project and the first complete statement of Socinian theology, built primarily around the preliminary work of Socinus and Statorius. Its authors were Valentine Smalcius, Hieronymus Moskorzowski, and John Völkel.

Smalcius was now the leading Socinian. He was a German convert, born at Gotha in 1572, who came to Poland from Strasburg. He was rector of the Minor Reformed Church's school at Smigiel, then minister at Lublin as successor to Czechowic, and finally at Raków from 1605 until his death in 1622. Moskorzowski was a distinguished layman noted for courteous controversy with Jesuits, and Völkel, another German, had been the amanuensis of Socinus.

A second Polish edition of the *Racovian Catechism* came off the press in 1619. In addition, between 1609 and 1684 there were eight Latin editions for general European use, plus three in Dutch and two each in German and English. More than is usually understood by a catechism, it was a comprehensive manual of Socinian doctrine in question and answer form. The first Latin edition, prepared by Moskorzowski in 1609, was dedicated to James I of England, but the gesture was not appreciated and it was burned by order of Parliament in April 1614.

The *Racovian Catechism* remained in circulation for 150 years. Though mild by comparison with later statements, it was regarded with neurotic fear by orthodox Protestants and repeatedly attacked and refuted. It presents Christianity primarily as a way of life demanding true knowledge of God and of his will revealed in Jesus Christ, with the key text being John 17:3, "And this is eternal life, that they may know you, the only true God, and Jesus Christ whom you have sent."* It maintains that Christ is a fitting object of prayer and adoration, though God is the primary object of worship and Christ secondary. The Virgin and the saints must not be invoked, but those who do not worship Christ are not truly Christian.

The *Catechism* also contains much discussion of the moral and civic duties of the Christian, with special emphasis on the necessity of a Christlike life. The Lord's Supper is the only true sacrament. Baptism is a sign of conversion and not suitable for infants. The Holy Spirit is essentially a divine power and not a person within the Godhead. Christ shows us how to turn to God. His sufferings and death are primarily an example and can reconcile us to God, but they do not atone for our sins, because God always forgives freely. The human will is free. Original sin is denied and predestination rejected. The Church is the whole company of those who confess sound doctrine.

---

* John 17:3, New Revised Standard Version.

24

The *Racovian Catechism* demonstrated a free and rational approach to scripture, with the main emphasis being on life and conduct. Other important works, including Christopher Ostorodt's *The Chief Points of the Christian Religion*, a popular presentation in German, and Völkel's *De vera religione (On True Religion)*, supplemented it. Ostorodt was a German Lutheran convert who settled in Poland and was responsible for introducing Socinianism in Holland.

The most successful period for the Minor Reformed Church was the first quarter of the seventeenth century. In spite of increasing threats of Jesuit persecution, the Polish Socinians mounted intense missionary and propagandist efforts, backed by a scholarly and controversial output from

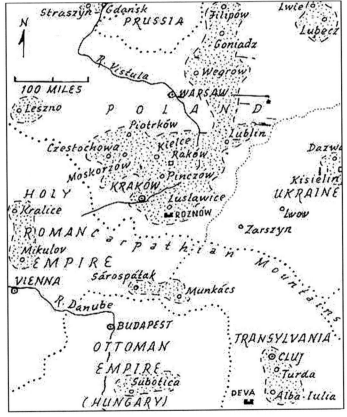

Map of Poland and surrounding areas of eastern Europe
circa 1600

their press at Raków. Although only the smallest of the denominations in Poland, the membership was cultured and influential, with considerable support from the nobility. Earlier estimates of some four hundred congregations are now known to be an exaggeration. In reality there were probably not more than 125, some of them short-lived, situated mostly in rural areas on aristocratic estates.

The Jesuits fiercely opposed Socinians in Poland in a long-term campaign involving the establishment of schools. The first king to come under Jesuit influence was Stephen Báthory, who reigned from 1574 till 1587. Persecution was intensified under his successor Sigismund III between 1587 and 1632. There was vigorous controversy between the Jesuits led by Peter Skarga and the Socinians led by Smalcius and Moskorzowski, with Skarga publishing *Shame of the Arians* in 1604, arguing that the Arians were no different from Muslims.

Persecution and Expulsion of the Socinians from Poland

Increasing polarization produced instances of mob violence and occasional judicial prosecution. The most conspicuous case was the burning at the stake in Warsaw of John Tyszkiewicz in 1611 for allegedly destroying a religious statue. A concerted Catholic and Calvinist attack on Socinians at Lublin in 1627 culminated in the complete suppression of the Minor Reformed Church in the town by 1638. At Raków, the same year, there were wild accusations of an impending assault that Socinians were expected to make on Catholicism, allegedly sparked off by a report of a schoolboy attack on a wayside shrine. This led to an official commission of investigation and,

The original Socinian parsonage at Raków
A Roman Catholic church now occupies the site of the nearby Meeting House.

ultimately, a formal sentence of condemnation against Raków by the Diet of Warsaw. Rigorously enforced, the Church, School and the Press were closed down. Teachers, ministers and all anti-Trinitarian inhabitants were forced to leave the town and a new Catholic church celebrating the suppression of the heresy was built on the site of the Socinian meetinghouse. The subsequent history of the town was one of steady decline.

The Trial of the Arians
Thomas Dolabelli's painting (before 1642) on the ceiling
of the episcopal palace at Kielce, Poland

With aristocratic patronage, Socinianism continued in Poland even after the suppression of Raków, though against a background of ever increasing persecution and a growing insistence that the *Pax Dissidentium* did not apply to the Arians. Some relief was anticipated when King Ladislas sponsored a *Colloquium Charitativum* at Toruń in 1644 to promote peace among Christians, but with the refusal of orthodox Protestants to participate the conference proved abortive. On the accession of John Casimir, himself a former Jesuit priest, in 1648, it was accepted that the *Pax Dissidentium* did not apply to Arians.

The final blow came with the formal proscription of Socinianism by the Diet of Warsaw in June 1658. All Socinians who did not renounce their faith within three years were required to go into exile and there was to be no public worship in the meantime. The time limit was then reduced to two years, and by the final date of 10 July 1660 the Polish Brethren faced an agonizing decision. Many conformed, with only a few hundred families accepting exile. A few found refuge in East Prussia, some in Lithuania, one or two in Switzerland, Holland or England, but the majority went to Kolozsvár where they were caringly received and settled by the Unitarian community under bishops Dániel Beke and Boldizsár Koncz. A smaller contingent made for Bethlen (Beclean), also in Transylvania, where with the patronage of Francis Bethlena they organized a Socinian congregation which lasted until the middle of the eighteenth century.

5

The Socinian Diaspora

The Socinian diaspora took almost every direction. Some went northeast to Lithuania, others to Switzerland, Holland or England. It was most prominent in the forty families, about two hundred refugees, who reached Kolozsvár (Cluj Napoca), Transylvania, in 1660.

It would be a mistake, however, to think that Unitarianism in Transylvania owes its origin to the Polish refugees. Their reason for heading toward Transylvania was the climate of religious toleration that already existed there, together with an established Unitarian community from whom they might expect a reception as kindred spirits, even though there were significant theological differences.

The Beginnings of Unitarianism in Transylvania

The community of Unitarian churches situated in the curve of the Carpathian mountains had developed at a similar time to the Minor Reformed Church in Poland, but was destined to outlive the Socinian community. It survives today as the Unitarian Church of Transylvania, the world's oldest organized Unitarian community, in what is now Romania. From earliest times it was a tightly organized, superintended church under the leadership of Francis Dávid, whose own spiritual development is neatly charted by his progress from Roman Catholic priest to Lutheran pastor, to bishop of the Reformed Church, and finally Unitarian bishop, or superintendent.

For several centuries Transylvania had been part of the Kingdom of Hungary, but in 1526 the Transylvanian nobles elected a king from among their own people. He was John Zápolya, under whose leadership the struggle against Hungary was maintained with the aid of the Sultan of Turkey, to whom they paid annual tribute. In all other respects they were an independent state until 1690, when the Diploma Leopoldinum integrated Transylvania into the Habsburg Empire. It was one of the many territorial annexations that have so tragically dogged Transylvania's history, not without implications for the life of its Unitarian churches, or their relations with Unitarians abroad.

John Sigismund, the Unitarian Monarch

John Zápolya had for his queen Isabella, daughter of King Sigismund I of Poland, who bore him a son in 1540 only a few days before he died. The boy, Prince John Sigismund, succeeded to the throne and has the distinction of being the only Unitarian monarch in history. There was, however, a rival king in Western Hungary, who was supported in his claim by the Pope, as John Sigismund was by the Sultan. The struggle was helped neither by John's infancy, nor the inexperience of the queen-mother, Isabella, who was acting as regent on her son's behalf. As a result, though John Sigismund was nominally King of Hungary, he held little more than Transylvania, and in 1570 it was agreed that he should relinquish his title to the Hungarian crown in return for the acknowledgment of Transylvania's independence.

It was during John Sigismund's reign that Unitarianism in Transylvania had its beginnings. As early as 1520 Luther's works had reached Transylvania, and monks returning from Wittenberg were preaching the Reformation doctrines. During his father's reign, laws had been passed to prevent the spread of heresy and two people were executed. But the legislation was not enforced because of preoccupation with matters of war, with the result that the Reformation spread more rapidly in Hungary than elsewhere. By 1535 the German Saxon settlers

John Sigismund
King of Hungary and Prince of Transylvania

had become Lutherans and the Hungarian-speaking Szeklers and Magyars soon followed, with only three of the nobles remaining faithful to the Catholic Church. Hungarian students went in large numbers to study at Wittenberg.

Protestantism was not quite so triumphal as this picture might suggest, for on 25 November 1556 the Diet of Kolozsvár allowed religious freedom for the old and new faith alike, by which was meant the Catholic and Lutheran religions. Moreover, this assurance was confirmed at the Diet of Torda (Turda) in June 1557, when legal toleration of both old and new religions was decreed by Isabella, "in order that each might hold the faith he wished, with the new rites as well as with the old, that this should be permitted him at his own free will." Except for the decree of 1526 in the Grisons, no previous law in Europe had enacted religious liberty even on this limited scale. Indeed, it was the confirmation and extension of this statute that eventually led to the historic enshrinement of religious liberty in the declaration at a further Diet held at Torda in 1568.

The Diet of 1557 also established a national synod for the discussion of the differences among Protestants concerning the Lord's Supper. The Lutheran doctrine, which held that the body and blood of Christ are present in the bread and wine, was widely recognized, but Calvin's Helvetic (Swiss) interpretation, that the bread and wine are only symbols, had reached Hungary circa 1550, when Reformed Churches were being founded. In due course the German Saxons remained Lutheran and the Magyars and Szeklers became Reformed. It was in one of these early discussions that the name of Francis Dávid was first heard, at this time defending the Lutheran point of view against the Reformed.

With debates about the Lord's Supper becoming so bitter, John Sigismund, anxious about peace and public order, summoned synods to see if harmony might be restored. At Torda in 1563 the decree of 1557 was confirmed, ordering "that each may embrace the religion that he prefers, without any compulsion, and may be free to support preachers of his own faith, and in the use of sacraments, and that neither party must do injury or violence to the other." The king also ordered, at the partial Diet of Torda held on 6 June 1563, that "in all those places where the old and new religions live together, they should share the Church building without offending each other."

Thomas Aran is generally regarded as the first exponent of Unitarianism in Hungary. In 1561 he was preaching specifically that Christ is not God, but only the Son of God, and a son of man; that the Holy Spirit is not God, but only the love of God; that there are not three persons in the Trinity; and that Christ is not the mediator between God and man. When he preached this at Debreczen, then as still today the major center of Hungarian Calvinism, he was opposed by Peter Mélius, the Reformed superintendent, and forced to defend himself in a debate lasting four days, when pressure was put on him by the civil powers to confess defeat and retract his opinions. Sometime later he again professed Unitarianism in Transylvania, but his defeat in the northern counties and in the great plain of Hungary meant only a very few churches adopted his views.

It was Francis Stancaro who was the real forerunner in Transylvania. He had entered Transylvania from Poland in 1553 and was forced to return five years later. Although he did not actually deny the Trinity or the deity of Christ, he was a crypto-Nestorian, radically separating the two natures of Christ, the divine and the human. For this he was bitterly opposed by both Peter Mélius and Francis Dávid, who at this time was still in his Lutheran phase.

George Blandrata

George Blandrata
court physician

Prophetic individuals could play a part in the developments, but the churches in Transylvania had, as they still have today, a semi-established character as "received religions," and it was unlikely they would make much headway without somebody of influence who had the ear of the Prince. George Blandrata (Biandrata), the court physician, was ideally placed to fulfill that role.

As already observed, Blandrata had been at the court of Queen Bona of Poland, who in 1544 sent him to Transylvania to attend her daughter Isabella, the mother of the young king, John Sigismund. After Isabella left Transylvania in 1551, he went to Italy, then to

Poland. He was recalled in 1562 to be court physician to John Sigismund, aged 23, who was now resident with his court at Gyulafehérvár (Alba Iulia). Keeping in touch with developments in Poland, Blandrata's influence on the young king was considerable, and it was he whom Sigismund sent to the Synod of Nagyenyed (Aiud) in 1564, where the controversy over the Lord's Supper led to the division of the Protestant churches into Lutheran and Reformed. It was here, for the first time, that Blandrata met Francis Dávid, who was to become the spiritual source of power that carried the Reformation forward in Transylvania as a Unitarian tendency.

6

Francis Dávid

The failure to resolve differences between the Lutherans and the Reformed (Helvetic) sacramentalists concerning the Lord's Supper led to a division of the two parties, at the king's bidding, into two separate churches, Lutheran and Reformed, each with its own bishop. It was at Nagyenyed (Aiud), where this partition took place, that Francis Dávid first met George Blandrata.

Francis Dávid was born at Kolozsvár (Cluj Napoca) circa 1520. His father, Hertel Dávid, was a prosperous German skin-dresser with a home within the city and a tannery beyond the walls. Shoemaking, an occupation where in all countries the work-

Francis Dávid
An imaginary portrait
by Prof. Dr. Gyula Lássló
No contemporary picture survives.

places are talking-shops that tend to radicalism, was also part of the trade. After his early education by Franciscans at Kolozsvár, Dávid went to the cathedral school at Gyulafehérvár (Alba Iulia), before studying briefly at Brassó (Braşov) and going on to the universities of Wittenberg and Frankfurt. Won over to Reformation doctrines, he identified first with the Lutherans, and then, after debates about the Lord's Supper, with the Reformed sacramentalists led by Peter Mélius. Eventually Dávid became bishop of the Reformed Church in Transylvania, the counterpart to Peter Mélius in Hungary, and at Blandrata's suggestion, the court preacher for John Sigismund.

Like his monarch, Dávid was influenced by Blandrata, but whereas Blandrata was cautious, Dávid was impatient to proclaim his Unitarian faith immediately. Their different temperaments later colored relationships between them, particularly concerning the adorantist controversy – whether worship should be offered to Christ – which ultimately led to Dávid's imprisonment.

By 1566 Dávid was openly preaching against the doctrine of the Trinity and gathering support from colleagues such as Stephen Basilius and Luke Égri. That year Peter Károli charged him with heresy and reported him to Peter Mélius. Dávid's response was to dismiss Károli, who left Kolozsvár to join forces with Mélius at Debreczen, where they solicited warnings from Calvin and Beza and sent them to the king. A prolonged and bitter controversy ensued, and for nearly five years there were regular, almost monthly debates about the doctrine of the Trinity at synod, diet, or in public forums.

The Edict of Torda

Public debate began at Gyulafehérvár (Alba Iulia) and adjourned to Torda (Turda) in 1566. Under the leadership of Dávid and Blandrata, the ministers who were present assented to the Apostles' Creed and adopted a statement of belief in the Trinity, which gave it a Unitarian interpretation, rejecting

"Faith is the gift of God"
Francis Dávid pleading for toleration at the Diet of Torda
The painting hangs in the museum at Torda (Turda)

35

the orthodox Athanasian doctrine as untenable. Then, a few weeks later, they went even further, apparently like Servetus and the Minor Reformed Church simply wishing to restore New Testament doctrine as a basis for Christian agreement.

In turn, in 1567 Peter Mélius called a synod at Debreczen, where liberals were not in the majority. Orthodox propositions were adopted and the ministers signed the Helvetic Confession recently adopted in Switzerland, as a further bar to heresy.

Meanwhile, in Transylvania the publication of *De Falsa et Vera Unius Dei Patris, Filii et Spiritus Sancti Cognitione* (*On False and True Knowledge of the One God, Father, Son, and Holy Spirit*) included eight coarse and offensive woodcuts which ridiculed the doctrine of the Trinity. More positively, its dedication, now known to be from the pen of Blandrata, urged the King to adopt peaceful even-handedness in matters of religion:

> We give eternal thanks to the almighty God, through his son, that he has given us a protector who believes that the truth of God is not spread with sword, fire and curse, but with strong arguments taken out of the Old and New Testaments. We beg your Highness to follow the advice of Gamaliel.

The work led to confirmation of the previous edicts of Torda of 1557 and 1564, and on 6-13 January 1568 to the Magna Carta of religion in Transylvania:

> Our Royal Highness, as he has decreed – together with the Diet – in the matter of religion, now again confirms that in every place the preachers shall preach and explain the gospel according to his understanding of it, and if the congregation like it, well; if not, no one shall compel them, but they shall keep the preachers whose doctrine they approve. Therefore none of the Superintendents or others shall annoy or abuse the preachers on account of their religion, according to the resolutions of the Diet, or to allow any to be imprisoned or be punished by removal from his post on account of his teaching, for faith is the gift of God. This comes from hearing, and hearing by the word of God.

Displeased by the turn of events, Mélius issued an invitation to his adversaries to a debate at Debreczen, but Blandrata advised the Transylvanian ministers to ignore it. The king himself then summoned a general synod of the ministers of both Hungary and Transylvania, to be held at his palace at Gyulafehérvár, to debate the Trinity. There were five debaters on the Unitarian side led by Dávid and Blandrata, and six on the Calvinist side led by Mélius. Beginning with prayers at five o'clock on the morning of 3 March 1568, it continued for ten days. Mélius appealed to the authority of the Bible, the creeds, the early Church Fathers and to orthodox theologians; Dávid to the Bible alone. On the ninth day the Calvinists asked to be excused from listening any further, whereupon the king pointed out that this would be admitting defeat, so they remained. Nothing new emerged to reconcile the parties, and the following day the king ended the debate, recommending that the ministers give themselves to prayer and refrain from unbecoming mutual abuse.

Although Blandrata had shown himself a poor debater and did not return to it again, the outcome of the Synod was generally regarded as a Unitarian victory. Dávid returned home to Kolozsvár and a hero's welcome. The stone from which he preached on that occasion is today housed in the entrance porch of the First Unitarian Church. Lutheran Saxons left the town, and for many years it was regarded as practically a Unitarian city.

Clausenburg (Kolozsvár/ Cluj Napoca)
A seventeenth-century engraving

Determined to carry the debate to the Hungarian people at large, Dávid obtained the king's permission to hold a synod at Nagyvárad (Oradea) on 20 October 1569 and the Calvinists were finally persuaded to attend. It did nothing to further the unity of the parties, and the king, having charged the Calvinists with evading the issue, closed it by siding with the Unitarians.

"The churches confessing one God, the Father"

The debate at Nagyvárad in 1569 marks the definitive schism between the Trinitarian and Unitarian sections of the Reformed church in Transylvania. From it, at first without any distinctive name, there emerged a well-organized people's church with Francis Dávid as a powerful spiritual leader and George Blandrata its shrewd spokesman at the royal court. Moreover, the king himself was of this church. Though not yet known as Unitarian, just before the synod of Nagyvárad Dávid and Blandrata had anonymously published a dual work, *De Regno Christi (On the Reign of Christ)* and *De Regno Antichristi (On the Reign of Antichrist)* in the name of "the Ministers and elders of the churches confessing one God, the Father." It was a period in which the Unitarian tendency advanced throughout Transylvania. By the time Dávid died there were over three hundred Unitarian congregations and by the end of the century more than 425, with some sixty more in Hungary.

In spite of this the Unitarians were troubled by the prospect that if the king died they would no longer retain the religious freedom enjoyed during his reign. Dávid therefore urged the king to act on the matter, and he was not slow to respond. At the Diet of Marosvásárhely (Tirgu Mures) early in 1571, the tone for the equality of the Catholic, Lutheran, Reformed and Unitarian faiths was established, though as "received religions" they were not formally enumerated until the Diet of Gyulafehérvár in 1595. So in theory they have remained until today, but now with the addition of the Romanian Orthodox Church.

The decision was timely, for two months later John Sigismund died. An accident involving a runaway horse, as he prepared to leave the royal seat to rest at one of his other castles, could not have helped his always precarious health, and he died on 15 March 1571, at thirty years of age.

Formal recognition of the Unitarian faith was also fortuitous because the hopes of the Unitarians that he would be succeeded by one of their own faith, Gáspár Békés, were not fulfilled. Stephen Báthory, a Catholic, was elected prince of Transylvania, and conditions became less favorable.

Under Báthory, Blandrata managed to retain his place at court. Had he not done so Unitarianism might have fared even worse. The situation, however, required the development of a *modus vivendi* with the ruling power. It was Blandrata's inability to control what were regarded as Francis Dávid's innovatory tendencies that resulted in the deterioration of their relationship, and eventually to Dávid's imprisonment and death. Dávid and his supporters argued that, on the contrary, their teachings were not innovations, but only the necessary development of doctrine as a result of study and reflection, which was the work of the ministry.

Although anti-Trinitarians no longer believed that Christ was equal with God, they had continued the practice of praying to him and, as we have seen, Socinus had maintained that the adoration of Christ was essential, otherwise Christians were no different from Muslims or Jews. Other scholars argued that, as scripture did not teach this, it ought to be given up. Already by 1572 Dávid himself was advocating the non-adorantist position. At Torda in 1578, with 322 ministers present, he spoke publicly against the worship of Christ and against infant baptism, as unscriptural.

Blandrata saw the danger of what he regarded as an extreme position, which would result in persecution if not the proscription of Unitarian opinion, and he urged Dávid to keep quiet. This he refused to do, arguing it would be hypocrisy. Blandrata then suggested that, to save the whole cause from ruin, it might be politic to have two or three ministers, those most zealous in the spreading of the new teaching, tried for heresy. It was an incredible strategy, which Dávid rejected as dishonorable. Blandrata's next ploy was to invite Socinus, then at Basel, to come to Transylvania to persuade Dávid. Traveling to Kolozsvár through Poland, Socinus lodged in Dávid's own house from autumn to spring conducting a running discussion on the subject of the worship of Christ. He warned that Dávid's innovations would lead back to Moses and Judaizing, but Dávid held to his opinion that the worship of Christ was idolatry.

The upshot was that Blandrata lost patience and refused any longer to defend Dávid with the regent Christopher Báthory, whose brother Stephen was now King of Poland. The relationship became one of bitter animosity. Dávid was brought before the courts, charged with introducing innovations, convicted, and imprisoned in the fortress at Déva (Deva) in June. He died there five months later on 15 November 1579.

From his position of influence at court Blandrata continued to reorganize the church. The administratively efficient but theologically conservative Demetrius Hunyadi was imposed as the new bishop. At the Synod of Kolozsvár in 1579 all the Unitarian ministers, except eighteen who were staunchly loyal to Dávid, reluctantly embraced Blandrata's *Disciplina Ecclesiastica* (*Church Discipline*), restoring infant baptism and a regular commemorative Lord's Supper.

Not surprisingly, Blandrata has not been highly regarded by later generations of Transylvanian Unitarians, who hold him responsible for Francis Dávid's imprisonment and death. However, a more critical approach to history is leading to the view that had it not been for his diplomacy, Francis Dávid's church might have suffered the same fate of extinction that befell the Minor Reformed Church in Poland.

7

Transylvanian Unitarianism
after Francis Dávid

For over a century after Francis Dávid's death, the Transylvanian church existed in a climate of oppression. Catholic tyranny ceased at the beginning of the seventeenth century, but it was followed, between 1604 and 1690, by Protestant opposition from the ruling Princes of Transylvania, who were of the Reformed faith. Then, between 1690 and 1781, the church was repressed by Austrian rule. Not until the Austro-Hungarian emperor Joseph II issued an Edict of Toleration in 1781 did conditions finally permit the church's renewal. In the meantime, Unitarian opinions often had to been glossed over, held secretly, or disguised using Trinitarian terminology.

Adopting the older interpretation of the term "counter-reformation," which suggests a movement in opposition to Protestantism rather than a parallel reforming movement within the Catholic Church, Professor János Erdő, who later became the tradition's twenty-ninth bishop, suggested that the sentence on Francis Dávid constituted the first victory of the counter-reformation.

Dávid's type of Unitarianism did not, however, end with his death, though it was deprived of its development and kept alive only in the secret writings of loyal ministers. Publicly the church adopted a conservative stance. Even while Dávid was still imprisoned in the fortress at Déva (Deva), under pressure from Blandrata and Demetrius Hunyadi, the Synod of Kolozsvár (Cluj Napoca)on 2 July 1579 adopted a creed which included acceptance of the divinity of Jesus and the worship of Christ. It also elected a council of twenty-four members to govern the church. In turn the council elected Hunyadi as bishop, an appointment confirmed by the regent Christopher Báthory.

Immediately after Dávid's death on 15 November 1579, Pál Kárádi, the Unitarian minister in Temesvár (Timisoara), wrote to his colleagues at Kolozsvár about his commitment to Francis Dávid's teaching, accusing Blandrata, Hunyadi and their party of being traitors. Shortly afterwards he led a secession of congregations in the Banat region of southwestern Transylvania to form a separate community of churches, of which he became the bishop.

Posthumous publication of Francis Dávid's defense, *Defensio Francisci Davidis*, provoked widespread disputations and these were followed by further output from Unitarian presses. Miklós Fazakas Bogati's translation of the *Psalms*, circulating in manuscript, provided a prototype for the first Transylvanian Unitarian hymnbook published sometime between 1602 and 1615.

The Accord of Dés

It was to curb these innovatory tendencies that in 1638 a Diet held at Dés (Dej) enacted the "Accord of Dés," which required Unitarians to worship and pray to Jesus, to baptize in the name of the Father, Son and Holy Spirit, and to publish only with the approval of the Prince. Moreover, it coerced the Unitarians to reintroduce infant baptism. Officially they signed a confession of beliefs, but beneath the surface several theological positions were adopted, ranging from conservative to radical non-adorantist. Resistance led to further oppression, the confiscation of churches and the prevention of Unitarian doctrinal clarification, which could not be resumed for nearly 150 years until the Edict of Toleration in 1781.

Under these strictures Transylvanian Unitarians probably avoided the worst aspects of religious persecution by identifying more closely with the adorantism, which, as we have seen, was a feature of the Polish Socinian refugee church in Transylvania.

The Austro-Hungarian Edict of Toleration

In 1781 the Edict of Toleration again made it possible for non-Catholic denominations to freely practice their faith and build churches. It also permitted the renewal of the Unitarian Church and the endowment of the Unitarian college at Kolozsvár, and led to the erection of a new church, which is still in use today for the congregation of Kolozsvár's first parish.

First Church, Kolozsvár (Cluj Napoca), erected 1792-1796
To the right is the Samuel Brassai Building, the headquarters of
the Transylvanian Unitarian Church

Late eighteenth-century renewal also made it possible for students for the ministry to revive their custom of studying at foreign universities. As a result they became aware of similar religious communities elsewhere, as others also became cognizant of their existence.

First International Contacts

The first reference to Transylvanian Unitarians in an English periodical occurred as an editorial notice in the *Monthly Repository* on 1 January 1811. It read:

A Unitarian Minister, who has bent his attention to the history of the Socinians on the Continent, would be glad to receive information concerning a pamphlet published about a dozen years ago, under the title of *A Statistical Account of the Unitarian Churches in Transylvania.*

No correspondent was able to identify this account, but six months later, on 26 June 1811, the Rev. Thomas Rees, in a sermon to the Southern Unitarian Book Society, gave the following information: "In Transylvania the congregations of the Unitarians at present amount to about 150 or 200, and the worshippers, it is supposed, to 60,000; and there is a Unitarian college at Clausenburg." (Clausenburg is the German rendering of the Hungarian Kolozsvár, as Cluj-Napoca is the Romanian.) It seems likely therefore that Rees knew of and was drawing on the *Statistical Account*.

A year later, in 1812, another entry in the *Monthly Repository*, by "Senex," referred to *The Religions of the World Displayed* by Robert Adam, minister of the Episcopal congregation at Blackfriars Wynd, Edinburgh, in which the author writes of *An Abstract of the faith and principles of the Unitarians of Transylvania*, published in 1787 by Professor Markos of the Unitarian College at Clausenburg. (The work referred to is now identified as Michael Szentábrahámi, *Summa Universae Theologiae Christiane secundum Unitarios,* 1787.) "Senex" concludes:

> May not some method be devised (perhaps through a mercantile medium) of opening a correspondence with Professor Markos, or some other respectable Unitarian in Transylvania, whereby we may know more of the circumstances of our Christian brethren in that remote country?

The enquiry, however, remained unanswered, and a few months later "Juvenis" wrote lamenting that the enquiry by "Senex" had called forth no account.

British awareness of Hungarian Unitarianism is again evident in 1818, in connection with the formation of Fellowship Fund societies, which, while primarily to encourage cooperation among the Unitarian churches in Britain, began to broaden their remit by establishing correspondence with Unitarian Christians in other parts of the world.

An account by John Kenrick in the *Monthly Repository* in 1820, "The History and actual condition of the Unitarians in Transylvania," written while Kenrick was a student at Göttingen University, provided information about church services, doctrine and the Unitarian college at Kolozsvár, arousing further interest and precipitating action.

On its fifteenth anniversary, 13 June 1821, The Unitarian Fund was informed that a Latin tract describing the opinions, history and institutions of English Unitarianism had been sent from London to Transylvania on 30 April 1821, accompanied by a letter signed by the Rev. W. J. Fox and the Rev. Robert Aspland, the secretaries of the Fund, and addressed to the Professor of Socinian Theology at Clausenburg. It was received there on 12 September and within a short time there was a warm response by Lazarus Nagy, a member of the Unitarian Consistory. This gave a short sketch of the Transylvanian Church, briefly stating its foundation and its position as a received church, and expressing brotherly feelings towards co-religionists in England.

Shortly after the receipt of this letter a longer and more complete statement of the position of the Transylvanian churches was received from George Sylvester, Professor of Theology at Kolozsvár, and published with the annual report of the Association for the Protection and Extension of the Civil Rights of Unitarians. A decade later even more detail was received by the Secretary of the British and Foreign Unitarian Association from Alexander Farkas, who in 1831 also traveled to the United States to establish connections with the American Unitarian Association.

The most detailed account relating to this British rediscovery of Eastern European anti-Trinitarian religion, which they had lost sight of in the persecutions which Socinians had suffered throughout Europe, came with John Relly Beard's *Unitarianism exhibited in its Actual Condition* (1846), to which John Paget, an English Unitarian, contributed an article based on his settlement in Transylvania, where he married a Hungarian baroness. As well as furthering the religious connections, Paget also made a significant contribution to Transylvanian agriculture by introducing new techniques.

In 1858, after a decade in which communications were virtually impossible as a consequence of the Hungarian Revolution of 1848, the

Bishop József Ferencz

Rev. Edward Taggart was sent to Transylvania to assess the situation as a representative of the British and Foreign Unitarian Association, but he died at Brussels on the return journey. It was perhaps the absence of his anticipated report that prompted further recollections from Paget in the *Christian Reformer* of that year. To recover information it felt must have been lost with Tagart's death, the Association in 1859 sent out the Rev. S. A. Steinthal. That year too, Aron Buzogány and József Ferencz, later to become bishop from 1876 to 1928, went to London for Unitarian meetings.

Relations with British and Americans were cordial and found expression in opportunities for Transylvanian students to study in Britain and the United States. Unitarian students from Transylvania were studying in London as early as 1830 and 1847. In 1860 Domokos Simén came to study at Manchester New College, then in its London phase. Sándor Kiss and Pal Benczédi were at the Unitarian Home Missionary College in Manchester in 1906 and 1907 respectively.

The last years of the century saw Transylvanian Unitarianism developing along lines closely parallel to the movements in Britain and the United States. At this stage there was probably greater organizational and doctrinal affinity than at any time before or since. For example, a Society of Unitarian Ministers was begun in 1896, while the Ministerial Fellowship in Great Britain was founded in 1899. There was mutual participation in the International Association for Religious Freedom founded in 1900.

8

The Twentieth Century

Between 1898 and 1901, the Transylvanian Unitarian Church built a fine new headquarters building. It was named after Sámuel Brassai, who in 1897 had bequeathed his library and property to the church. The first decade of the century saw the establishment of a monthly journal *Unitarian Church* and a periodical *Unitarian Pulpit* to support preaching activity.

In 1910 the four-hundredth anniversary of the birth of Francis Dávid was celebrated by the placing of a plaque in the dungeon of the Castle at Déva (Deva). Popular celebrations at this time also led to the first publication of the annual *Unitarian Christian Popular Calendar*.

Transylvanian Unitarian students continued to study in Britain and the United States. Sándor Kiss was at the Unitarian Home Missionary College in Manchester in 1906, as was Pal Benczédi in1907. The establishment of the Sharpe Hungarian Scholarship at Manchester in 1911 promised further development of the scheme, but the outbreak of World War I was again an obstacle to making contacts with overseas Unitarian movements, reminiscent of the difficulties surrounding the revolutions of 1848. Although József Sigmond had been selected as the first recipient of the Sharpe Hungarian Scholarship, the war made it impossible for him to travel and the scheme could not be implemented until hostilities ended, when Dénes Lőrinczy came for two years.

The Treaty of Trianon

As part of the redrawing of borders at the end of World War I, the Treaty of Trianon of 1920 made Transylvania a part of Romania. This associated it with an eastern-looking culture, which was regarded as very different from that of countries situated to the west. The annexation was deeply resented and has been ever since. There was a long history of tension and conflict between the Hungarians and the Romanians. Moreover, the presence in Romania of a large Gypsy population, at odds with both the Romanian majority and the Hungarian minority, has added to the complexity of the tensions under which Transylvanian Unitarians have striven to maintain their religious and cultural identity.

After 1920 the Unitarian community was not only a religious minority, as it had always been, but a national minority as well. Their shared plight provided a degree of cohesion between the Unitarians and the Hungarian-speaking Reformed and Lutheran churches in Transylvania, in the interest of the preservation of Hungarian culture.

The Romanian government restricted the cultural and religious liberties of the Hungarian minority, including rights of public worship and assembly. Schools, colleges, and other church property were confiscated. Forests and farms in church ownership were especially targeted in the redistribution of land for agrarian reform.

Overseas contacts were vigorous in the inter-war years. Students were at Manchester College Oxford and Unitarian College Manchester, and the five-year-long peregrination of Francis Balázs in Britain and the United States epitomizes the usefulness of international contacts. Balázs returned to the pastoral ministry in Transylvania, giving remarkable spiritual leadership to his colleagues.

Francis Balázs

During World War II, Romania was allied with Germany, and contacts were of necessity again suspended, with one or two students, Gabor Kereki of the Hungarian branch and Gyula Benedek, finding themselves on the wrong side of the geographical divide. After a period of Hungary and Transylvania being reunited under German rule, Transylvania was returned to Romania at the end of the war.

The Communist Era

During the post-World War II Communist era, the Romanian constitution and the 1949 Law of Religions placed narrow restrictions on all aspects of church activity. An early victim was the Academy of Unitarian Theology, which in 1948 the State directed to be incorporated into the United Protestant Theological Institute, with university status. Henceforth, Unitarian ministerial training took place ecumenically alongside students preparing for the ministries of the Hungarian-speaking Reformed and Lutheran churches.

In the parishes, religious teaching was limited and the education of the church's young people prohibited; meetings were monitored by the State's regional supervisors; ministers' conferences were proscribed; and reports of district assemblies had to be submitted to regional offices, with the insulting requirement in some regions that they must be in Romanian rather than Hungarian. The work of the ministry was severely restricted and there were no opportunities for engagement in public life. Where ministers were too vocal in their criticisms of the regime, or too strident in the promotion of Hungarian culture, they were tried and incarcerated on trumped-up charges. The Hungarian Uprising in 1956 made matters worse, as the Romanian authorities feared it might encourage revolt among the Hungarian diaspora in the neighboring regions. Reminiscent of the *modus operandi* adopted under Austro-Hungarian rule, Transylvanian preachers at this stage sought to encrypt their Sunday sermons in the "flower language" of the pulpit. As Imre Gellérd's scholarly *History of Transylvanian Unitarianism through Four Hundred Years of Sermons* illustrates, Hungarian homiletic is generally more poetic than in Britain or America.

Between 1958 and 1964, eighteen Unitarian ministers and theological students, and one lay official, the librarian and archivist of the Unitarian library, were sentenced to imprisonment for terms between one and twenty-five years. For some this meant hard labor in prisons located in the Danube delta with its unhealthy climate. The incarceration of the three who were staff at the Protestant Theological Institute and four of their students resulted from the seizure at the Romanian border of sermons by Imre Gellérd, to which annotations had been added by others, and which were interpreted, on slender grounds, as being subversive. Release came after five years, when in 1964, under international political pressure, Gheorghe Gheorghui-Dej, the Romanian Communist Party's General Secretary, pardoned all political prisoners. It was not an amnesty, and an additional five years' deprivation of civil rights was necessary before formal rehabilitation could be granted. In Gellérd's case this was not until May 1975.

It does not appear that all the ministers who later suffered imprisonment were at first opposed to a Communist regime. Imre Gellérd, on whom attention has been focused by his daughter's account of his sufferings, was a Marxist scholar and member of the Communist Party, seeing in it ideals which corresponded with his Christian understanding. It was their opposition to the subsequent adoption of Soviet totalitarianism and their resistance to the implementation of collective farming, so agriculturally and socially inappropriate to the Transylvanian landscape, that later brought them into conflict with State authority. Another factor was the suppression of the traditions of the Hungarian minority and the confiscation of the schools and properties by which they could be maintained.

Contacts with Unitarians abroad were not entirely forbidden, but they were severely restricted. A very few students were allowed to take up scholarships at Unitarian College Manchester, or at Meadville/Lombard or Starr King theological schools in the United States. In 1968 an international gathering was held in Transylvania to celebrate the 400th anniversary of the Edict of Torda. There were, however, some setbacks. After the defection to the United States of Zoltán Harkó, a Sharpe Scholar at Unitarian College Manchester in 1969, another permit was not granted to a student until 1985. Nonetheless, Bishop Lajos Kovács, together with Bishop József Ferencz of Hungary, grandson of the first Bishop Ferencz, were frequent visitors to the British General Assembly's meetings, albeit circumspect about general conversation and confining their participation to the delivery of formal greetings.

Under these restrictive conditions, between 1948 and 1989, the Transylvanian Unitarian Church perceived itself as a "fortress" church. As a product of the Reformation, it found an image and inspiration in Martin Luther's hymn, *Ein Feste Burg*. Indeed, Dr. Arpád Szabó, the present bishop, just prior to speaking about the Romanian situation at a conference of the British Ministerial Fellowship, asked for confirmation that "burg" translated into English as "fortress," or possibly "castle." Besieged, the churches became centers for the loyalty of the "believers," as the members are called. They found secret ways of communicating. Yet despite economic hardships there was faithful support for the Church and its ministers.

December 1989

The collapse of the repressive Ceausescu regime in December 1989 promised great changes for Transylvanian Unitarians, as it did for the Hungarian-speaking minority generally. There is, however, a reluctance to describe the events of December 1989 as a "revolution," on the grounds that, as one senior minister has written, the "level of improvement that society had expected did not take place." While there has been some improvement in living standards, the broader picture is of unemployment and economic hardship, and the internal political choices continue to be between atheistic Communism and rampant nationalism. The parties representing these views favor Romanian identity and culture, continuing and exacerbating the grievances the Hungarian-speaking minority has felt since the annexation of Transylvania by the Trianon agreement in 1920. The Hungarians find a small voice in the Democratic Alliance of Hungarians in Romania and a few ministers are involved in its leadership, though some argue that persons who were previously executives of the Communist Party lead it.

The Reconstruction of Transylvanian Unitarian Church Life

The events of 1989 brought a relaxation of the persecution Unitarians had suffered for more than forty years, beginning with the establishment of the Soviet system in 1948. In *Confessions about Ourselves*, edited by Mózes Kedei, the ministers described how life had been for them before 1989 and the fresh opportunities it gave for their personal lives, their ministries, and their Church.

After 1989 there was freedom to speak more openly. Ministers could participate in civic events and were invited to do so. The work of the ministry became more demanding, since it was no longer restricted. Yet with the relaxation of repression and the new opportunities for people to advance themselves economically, there has been a loss of the cohesiveness that held the "fortress" church together. One minister wrote of the bitterness he feels "over the clear perishing of community ...What the previous regime did not succeed in doing with all its atheism – to crush cohesion of the souls, to dissolve our unity and to achieve these by our disappearance – selfishness, bewildered by the desire of getting rich quickly, will fulfill."

No longer restricted to merely conducting worship, ministers faced new tasks and new challenges. The Consistory sought and still seeks the recovery of buildings, land and forests confiscated by the State. It also faced the task of re-establishing trust among its ministers and members, which had suffered under the strains of loyalty to principles and the necessity of a *modus vivendi* with the repressive regime.

Bishop Lajos Kovács, who had succeeded Dr. Elek Kiss in the leadership of the Church during this difficult period in 1972, died in 1994 and was succeeded by Bishop János Erdő, who had long been respected for his learning and spirituality. On his death in 1996, Dr. Arpád Szabó was elected bishop, thirtieth in line from Francis Dávid.

Opportunities for Transylvanian and Hungarian Unitarians to travel abroad changed dramatically after 1989, as did freedom to enter Romania. A highlight of the British General Assembly in 1990 was the reception given to Dr. János Erdő, later Bishop Erdő, and Bishop Ferencz, who were able to make their responses openly. By the end of the following year arrangements were in place for the revival of scholarships for theological students, with József Kászoni, minister of Homoródszentmárton (Sinmartin), attending Unitarian College, Manchester. Since then there has been a regular flow of students to Unitarian College Manchester, Harris Manchester College Oxford, and colleges in the United States. The Hungarian Unitarian tradition of sending students to study abroad, from its beginnings in the seventeenth century, has recently been fully chronicled by Sandor Kovács in *Unitarian to the Core*, edited by Leonard Smith. The changes also allowed an increase in the number of students preparing for the ministry, with a higher percentage of women amongst them.

In the reverse direction, Austin Fitzpatrick, on behalf of British Unitarians, took the initiative in arranging for economic aid to be provided, with truckloads of supplies being sent by road. Americans too, from a greater distance, were not slow to provide financial support, and later to develop the Partner Church Program, to some extent replicating the arrangements of the 1920s. They also funded and supplied teachers of English for the Unitarian students at the Protestant Theological Institute. Another scheme made possible by international support was the addition of a further storey at the Sámuel Brassai Unitarian headquarters, which also serves as the High School, to accommodate theological students in single rooms, instead of the dormitories previously used.

The new freedoms have also brought opportunities for Transylvanians to emigrate to metropolitan Hungary and beyond. When this occurs it usually means a loss of younger people. One minister writes of the loss of thousands. While this may be true, it seems likely that the Romanian church's losses may be Hungary's gain. In 1925 Earl Morse Wilbur gave the number of adherents as 80,000, with ten per cent of them in Hungary. This figure is still being quoted for Romania. However, the declarations of religious affiliation, which are required for Romanian Census purposes, revealed 63,849 for the year 2002. The Hungarian branch, independent since 1949, now claims to have 25,000 members, though verbal reports suggest this may be an exaggeration. Precise figures are difficult to come by, since it is possible that there are many Transylvanian Unitarian exiles now living in Hungary whose active connection with the churches has lapsed.

The Unitarian Church of Hungary

The Unitarian Church in metropolitan Hungary has a common ancestry with the Transylvanian Church. The cohesive document of the Unitarian churches of Transylvania and Hungary is the *Hungarian Unitarian Catechism*, revised by each church to reflect its own needs. The Transylvanian version begins with the question, "What is Religion?" The answer is: "Religion is love toward God and toward our neighbor." The work is divided into nine sections: 1. Concepts, 2. God, 3. The Child of God, 4. Jesus, 5. The Holy Spirit, 6. The Unitarian Church, 7. Sin and Repentance, 8. Eternal Life and 9. Liturgical Service, being an exposition of Baptism and the Lord's Supper, the quarterly celebration of which is a central feature of the worship in Romania and Hungary.

In the sixteenth century there were more than 100 congregations in the territory of present-day Hungary. However, after the Roman Catholic counter-reformation, Unitarians could only be found in Transylvania, until, following the revolution in 1848-49, they were able to return to Budapest and elsewhere in Hungary.

The Unitarian Church of Hungary was an integral part of the Transylvanian church until Transylvania became part of Romania in 1920. From 1902 it was organized as an independent district with its own bishopric. An impressive headquarters, incorporating Budapest's first church, was erected with British and American support in the early years of the twentieth century. Its complete separation from the much larger Transylvanian Church dates from the end of World War II.

Headquarters of the Unitarian Church of Hungary, Budapest

Arguably, the Hungarian branch suffered less under the strictures of Communism than did the Transylvanian Unitarians, but it was at the cost of being coerced into signing an "agreement" to work with the State, which the Reformed and Unitarian Churches did on 7 October 1948, followed by the Lutheran and Jewish communities two months later. The Church is today grouped into twelve congregations and twenty-one fellowships.

Norbert Čapek and the Czech Unitarian Association

The history of Unitarianism in Poland, Transylvania, and Hungary does not entirely exhaust the locations where it has emerged in continental Europe, but in other places it is a relatively modern phenomenon.

In 1918 the Republic of Czechoslovakia declared its independence from the Austro-Hungarian Empire. As an expression of the new country's national identity, a million Roman Catholics seceded to form the Czechoslovak Church. Although episcopal in polity and liturgically traditional, the church was theologically liberal. Consequently the International Association for Liberal Christianity and Religious Freedom adopted it, a relationship that lasted until 1963.

In 1921 Norbert Čapek, a former Czech Baptist minister who had spent several years in the United States, returned to Czechoslovakia. In 1922 he established an avowedly Unitarian church, which reported 3,395 members in 1932. The Czechoslovak Unitarian Association was founded in 1930. Čapek was killed by the Nazis at the Dachau concentration camp in November 1942.

Čapek is best known as the originator of the Flower Communion, which he developed for his new congregation in 1923. It is celebrated in Unitarian and Unitarian Universalist churches around the world. As Čapek explained:

> Each of us is choosing a different flower, and that one speaks for us. The vase is again a symbol for us. For us in our Unitarian brotherhood, the vase is our church organization. We need it to help us share the beauties, but also the responsibilities, of communal life. In the proper community, by giving the best that is in us for the common good, we grow up and are able to do what no single person is able to do. Each of us needs to receive in order to grow up, but each of us needs to give something away for the same reason.

Today the Czech Unitarian Association is a member of the International Association for Religious Freedom and the International Council of Unitarians and Universalists, and has congregations in Prague, Brno, Plzen, and Liberec.

Other Unitarian Movements in Europe

The first Norwegian Unitarian church was founded in the 1890s by Hans Tambs Lyche and Kristofer Janson, two ministers who, like Norbert Čapek, had lived in the United States. Unitarian societies were founded in Sweden during the 1870s and 1880s. None of these societies has survived, but Unitarianism was reintroduced in both countries during the 1980s. There has been a Unitarian society in Copenhagen, Denmark since 1901.

The largest organization of European Unitarians outside the traditional Unitarian regions of Poland, Transylvania, and Hungary is the Deutscher Unitarier Religionsgemeinschaft (German Unitarian Religious Community). It was organized in 1950, but traces its origin to the "Free Protestant" movement of the 1870s. It has about 1500 members and friends in 23 congregations and a youth fellowship.

The new internationalism of the post-World War I period saw the development of small groups in other parts of Europe, including Bulgaria and Italy, though some were only short-lived. More recently, the International Council of Unitarians and Universalists, founded in 1995, has encouraged the formation of new groups in Latvia, Finland, Russia and Spain, as well as the revival of Unitarianism in Poland.

PART 2

GREAT BRITAIN

9

Origins: Native or Exotic?

Soon after British and Transylvanian Unitarians rediscovered each other in the early nineteenth century, a debate arose concerning the emergence of Unitarianism in Great Britain. Was it a question of anti-Trinitarian ideas spreading geographically across Europe to take root in the British Isles, or did they arise independently in Great Britain? Was it native, or exotic?

In his *Sources of English Unitarianism*, the French historian Gaston Bonet-Maury favored the idea of anti-Trinitarian opinions having been brought across the English Channel, either by Socinian missionaries, or in published works circulating from the Minor Reformed Church's press at Raków. The British Unitarian historians J. J. Tayler and Alexander Gordon argued to the contrary, that Bonet-Maury was exaggerating his claims and that the proto-Unitarian John Biddle reached his theology without reference to Socinian books, solely from reading the New Testament, where he found no evidence of the doctrine of the Trinity. Whatever the merits of these arguments, the likely bias of the British historians in a period when Imperialism was at its height needs to be remembered.

To support his view, Bonet-Maury emphasized the presence of Socinian ideas amongst continental refugees who were members of the Strangers' Church in London. Moreover, the case of Paul Best is frequently cited to explain the passage of anti-Trinitarian, or proto-Unitarian views across the English Channel. Best, a member of Parliament, had adopted Unitarian opinions in the course of his travels in Poland and Transylvania. Betrayed by a clergyman friend with whom he had privately shared them on his return to England, he was brought before the House of Commons and imprisoned for blasphemy.

The facts probably incorporate both opinions, but the debate is nonetheless stimulating for any consideration of early British Unitarian developments. Biddle may indeed have reached his conviction independently, but Socinian works were certainly in circulation in England and it is unlikely that he could have been entirely unaware of them. He did, in fact, translate one of them from Latin to English, though this may have been after he had independently reached his Unitarian point of view.

Pre-Reformation Influences

There were native British influences predating the Reformation, which, while not specifically leading to Unitarianism, paved a way for it. For example, the Lollards, led by John Wycliffe, were reformers before the Reformation, and Wycliffe has picturesquely been described as its Morning Star. Their insistence on the priority of scripture over other authorities and their efforts to make it available in the vernacular, through Wycliffe's own translations, were important developments. Coupled not only with the right, but also the obligation of private judgment, they presaged the Reformation in Britain, as Jan Hus did in Bohemia a century before Luther's revolt in Germany.

Lollardy was not itself anti-Trinitarian, but measures to restrict its influence unwittingly drew attention to anti-Trinitarianism. A Bill for

John Wycliffe

the imprisonment of heretics was introduced in Parliament in 1382, followed in 1401 by the even sterner measure *De Heretico Comburendo (On the Burning of Heretics)*. This Act, which was used to impose death by burning, particularly against anyone who denied the Trinity, was not finally repealed until 1677. When Reginald Pecock, the bishop of St Asaph, attempted to halt the Lollard movement on its own terms by setting aside ecclesiastical infallibility and appealing to scripture and reason, he too unwittingly brought upon himself charges of heresy and his predicament anticipated later controversies about Reason versus Scripture.

Early British Anti-Trinitarians

A few anti-Trinitarians contemporaneous with the Lollards were arraigned before the courts for doctrinal heresy. William Sawtrey, a priest at Kings Lynn, was charged with denying infant baptism and transubstantiation, and refusing to adore the cross. Convicted of heresy, he later recanted but was convicted again and burned at the stake at Smithfield on 20 March 1401, eight days before the passage of *De Heretico Comburendo*. It is the first known incidence of the death penalty for religious opinions in England, though even earlier, in 1327, Adam Duff O'Toole, who denied the incarnation and the doctrine of the Trinity, was burned at Dublin.

Bonet-Maury's contention that the origins of British Unitarianism lie in continental European sources rested principally on the presence in England of anti-Trinitarian tendencies amongst exiles that made up the congregation of the Strangers' Church, which gathered at the church of Austin Friars. In 1550 it was believed there were 3,000 foreign Protestant refugees in London, chiefly from the Low Countries, but also from France, Italy and Spain. They included John Laski (a Lasco) and Bernadino Ochino, not yet anti-Trinitarian but leaning in that direction. Others associated with the émigré congregation were Giacomo Aconzio, who was denied communion on account of his alleged Arianism; Cassiodoro de Reyna, a follower of Servetus; George van Parris, a surgeon from Mainz, burned for Arianism at Smithfield on 25 April 1551; and Laelius Socinus, uncle of Faustus Socinus. The presence in England of these influential figures associated with European developments lends some credibility to Bonet-Maury's thesis. However, his opponents argued that, speaking other languages, the foreign exiles were unlikely to have had much influence amongst the English. This may have been true at popular levels, but arguably less so amongst scholars who conversed in Latin.

Opponents of Bonet-Maury's thesis also held that there were anti-Trinitarians in England before the organization of the foreign congregations. John Assheton, a Lincolnshire clergyman, is an example. After a trial before Archbishop Cranmer for denying the doctrine of the Trinity, which he declared to be the work of Athanasius, and maintaining that the Holy Spirit was not God but only a certain power of the Father, he recanted his opinions on 28 December 1548. Jesus Christ, he maintained, though conceived of the virgin Mary, was truly a prophet of God, a holy prophet but not God himself. As for the atonement, Assheton asserted that the fruit of Jesus's death was that it brought us to knowledge of God's power, thus rescuing us from the condition of being strangers to God – a view very similar to that of the Socinians.

A few years after Assheton's recantation Patrick Pakingham was burned at Uxbridge as an Arian in 1555. With Christopher Vitells he appears to have been a member of the Family of Love (Familists), a society with origins in Munster, which included Anabaptists of an anti-Trinitarian type. The distinction of being the last two people to be executed for religious opinions in England rests, however, with Bartholomew Legate, burned at Smithfield, and Edward Wightman, at Lichfield, in 1612, both anti-Trinitarians.

The truth probably lies neither entirely on one side or the other. The English Bible with no evidence of the Trinity in it, the presence of the Strangers' Church in London, the anti-Trinitarianism of a few English Anabaptists and the spread of Socinian books all played some part.

Of the works disseminating from the Minor Reformed Church's press at Raków, the most important was the *Racovian Catechism* of 1605, which was a summary of Socinian teaching and theology. Making its appeal directly to the Bible, it asserted the benevolence of God and rejected the deity of Christ, though he is adopted by God and is therefore a fit object of worship. It argued for tolerance and the reduction of the necessities of salvation to a few basic essentials. It received widespread attention in England in 1609, with the publication of the first Latin edition dedicated to King James I.

The greatest influence of Socinian thought in this period was not however on the sectaries, but upon the Latitudinarian party within the Church of England. The term Latitudinarian derives from latitude-men, who adopted a more liberal approach to matters of faith. For example, Lord Falkland, John Hales and particularly William Chillingworth were advocates of tolerance and religious freedom.

John Biddle

Chief among English anti-Trinitarians was John Biddle, who has been called the "Father of English Unitarianism." Born at Wooton-under-Edge, Gloucester, in 1615, the son of a wool merchant, he graduated at Magdalen Hall, Oxford in 1638, before returning to his home county as master of the St Mary de Crypt Grammar School in Gloucester. Biddle claimed to have reached his anti-Trinitarian, proto-Unitarian position solely by reading the Bible, before he was aware of any Socinian literature. Doubting that the doctrine of the Trinity had any basis within it, in 1644 he composed a short theological statement in which he sought to establish the unity of God by showing from scripture that the Holy Spirit is not God but only a manifestation of God.

A more detailed exposition of Biddle's theology was his *XII Arguments Drawn out of the Scripture: Wherein the commonly received Opinion touching the Deity of the Holy Spirit, is clearly and fully refuted,* published in 1647.

For his views Biddle suffered intermittent imprisonment until released under the Act of Oblivion of 1652, a general conciliatory pardon of all but a few crimes, passed by Cromwell's parliament at the end of the Civil War. He was at liberty between February of that year and December 1654.

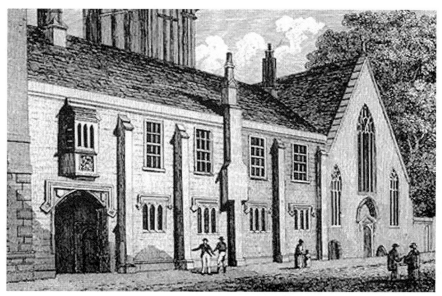

St Mary de Crypt Grammar School, Gloucester, where John Biddle was Master

During this period he organized a congregation in London, probably the first avowedly anti-Trinitarian church in Britain. Its members called themselves Biddellians, Socinians, or Mere Christians. It was perhaps in response to the needs of this congregation that his *Twofold Catechism* was published in 1654, the most radical attack on orthodox Christianity ever to have appeared in Great Britain.

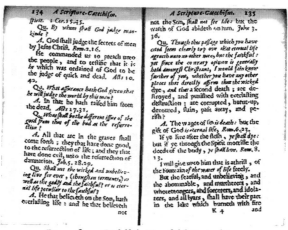

Pages from Biddle's Twofold Catechism

Imprisoned again, he escaped the death penalty through the intervention of the Lord Protector Oliver Cromwell, who provided a pension and banished him to the Isles of Scilly. Released after three years, Biddle endeavored to resume the London meetings, only to be incarcerated again. Freed once more, he died shortly afterwards, on 2 September 1662, as a result of a disease contracted in prison.

A summary of Biddle's views was given by Sir Peter Pett in his *The Happy Future State of England*, 1688: Biddle maintained that salvation consisted of obedience to the commands of God and Christ; that justifying faith can be acquired by man's natural abilities; that faith can never be contrary to or above reason; that there is no original sin; that Christ was not exalted after the Ascension and that his death is not an act of satisfaction. He held to the general Protestant principle that no authority should be ascribed to the Early Church Fathers, or to Church Councils.

10

Protestant Nonconformity

The Act of Uniformity 1662

The Restoration of the Monarchy in 1660 ended all hopes of any radical reform of the Church of England. Two years later, only a month before John Biddle died in September 1662, the Act of Uniformity was imposed on the nation in an attempt to settle the diverse forms of religious practice, even while it could not realistically eradicate theological differences. The measure was coupled with the introduction of the *Book of Common Prayer*, to whose contents all clergy were required to declare their "unfeigned assent and consent" and to read from it on or before St. Bartholomew's Day, 24 August 1662. Failure to comply would result in them being deprived of their parochial benefices and college fellowships.

Popular tradition has long held that some 2,000 of the ablest Puritan ministers were ejected, possibly a tenth of all the Church's clergy. Research has revealed that the figure was nearer to 1,700, representing all deprivations between 1660 and 1662. About 700 were put out in 1660, when Royalist clergy deprived during the Commonwealth reclaimed their livings, in turn putting out the Commonwealth's nominees, now somewhat derisively described as interlopers or titular rectors. Another 900 were put out in 1662. In the universities a further 150 were deprived of college fellowships.

For the history of English Protestant Nonconformity, the events of 1662 and the Great Ejection were decisive and assumed heroic significance. For many years memories of the enforcement of the Act and the sufferings it caused were solemnly remembered by designating 24 August 1662 as Black Bartholomew's Day.

Moreover, a raft of other penal measures, collectively known as the Clarendon Code, which enabled magistrates to enforce the legal requirements, supplemented the Act of Uniformity. Chief of these were the Conventicle Act of 1664 and the Five Mile Act of 1665; the former forbidding any religious meetings of more than five persons, except for worship according to the usages of the Church of England, and the latter preventing ejected clergy from passing within five miles of any parish where they had been the incumbent, or of any Corporation town, thus reducing their influence.

The immediate result was the cessation of doctrinal development among nonconforming clergy. Dissenters were now preoccupied with survival and the evasion of legal penalties. In any case, very few of them were doctrinally heretical; their objections concerned matters of practice, rather than belief. For example, as Puritans they were opposed to Prayer Book worship with its prescribed liturgy, the making of the sign of the cross in baptism, the wearing of a surplice and the use of the ring in marriage services.

The Trinitarian Controversy in the Church of England

Doctrinal debate continued, however, in the Church of England. A controversy concerning the doctrine of the Trinity began with the publication of *The Naked Gospel* by Arthur Bury of Exeter College, Oxford, in which he rejected the doctrine as no part of the original gospel.

As a result of collaboration between Stephen Nye, the rector of Little Hormead, Hertfordshire, and the layman Thomas Firmin, a series of Unitarian Tracts, six volumes in all, was published between 1691 and 1703.

In 1687, Nye published anonymously, at Firmin's request, *A Brief History of the Unitarians, called also Socinians,* consisting of four letters that he had sent to Firmin. After what was indeed a very brief history, the remainder of his book was an exposition of Unitarian doctrines and a discussion of the scripture texts on which they were founded. It went unnoticed at the time, but later attracted much attention and started the Trinitarian Controversy in the Church of England, which lasted for about a century.

Thomas Firmin, the main promoter of the tracts, was a wealthy philanthropic mercer. Under the influence of Biddle he came to distrust almsgiving and to attack the causes of social distress by economic effort, thus providing an early example of Unitarian concern with social issues. Firmin shared Biddle's views of the Trinity and the anthropomorphic view of God which was current among Socinians, but he became Sabellian under the influence of Stephen Nye.

Nye's usage of the term Unitarian, in 1687, was once thought to be the earliest in English, though it has since been identified in Henry Hedworth's *Controversie Ended*, 1672/3. Another early incidence of it in Britain is a Latin *Epistle* of 1682, discovered in 1892 by Alexander Gordon in the Tillotson archive at the Library of Lambeth Palace. This strange text is an address by "two philosophers" claiming to represent "the sect of Christians that are called Unitarians," to Ahmet Ben Ahmet, the Ambassador of the King of Morocco to the English court. Its authors commend themselves to the ambassador by asserting the doctrinal similarities between Unitarianism and Islam concerning the unity of the Godhead, but it has no real significance for the further development of British Unitarianism.

Nonconformity under Persecution and Indulgence

While loyal conforming Latitudinarians were engaged in the Unitarian Controversies, between the Ejection in 1662 and the Act of Toleration in 1689 Nonconformity existed under persecution relieved by occasional Acts of Indulgence. For example, in 1672 licenses could be obtained for services to be held in registered houses and for licensed ministers to preach, though the following year they were withdrawn and persecution was renewed.

Several Unitarian congregations have oral traditions of secret meetings being held in remote locations. At Walmsley Chapel, Egerton, Lancashire, a painting hangs in the Sunday school depicting Yearnsdale, a nearby moorland hollow where sentinels were set and worship was held in defiance of the Conventicle Act.

The Toleration Act

After the passage of the Toleration Act of 1689, secrecy was no longer necessary, though toleration did not extend either to Roman Catholics or anyone who denied the Trinity. John Locke's *Letters concerning Toleration* (1689, 1690 and 1692) helped to promote the general spirit of religious liberty and free enquiry, but the major disabling measures, which prevented Dissenters from holding public office, remained in place and continued to be restrictive until the repeal of the Test and Corporation Acts in 1828, and minor ones as late as 1880. These were sometimes circumvented by the practice of Occasional Conformity, taking the sacrament once a year at the parish church to qualify for public office, or a commission in the services.

An immediate consequence of the Toleration Act was that many Roman Catholics conformed while Dissenters leaning toward Unitarian opinions held their views cryptically within the framework of orthodox Protestant Dissent.

The Act also permitted the building of meetinghouses and chapels. In the two decades which followed, from 1689 to 1710, a thousand or so Presbyterian, Independent, Baptist and Quaker places of worship were erected. Their frequently secluded locations has resulted in conjecture that they were remotely sited to avoid attention, but to the contrary it is possible to find several prominently placed in town centers. Wherever they are the modest architecture lends weight to the view that their builders thought of them as only temporary dwellings, until a hoped-for broadening of the Established Church enabled dissenters to be comprehended.

Cohesion of the Dissenting Interest

If the passage of the Toleration Act was a result of the failure to enforce uniformity of religion, any continuing hopes that Nonconformists had of eventually being embraced within the Established Church died with it. The consequence was that some abortive attempts were made to achieve the cohesion of the Dissenting interest by uniting the two main nonconformist bodies, the Presbyterians and Independents.

The first of a long series of moves to this end came in 1690 with the foundation of a Common Fund managed by representatives of both denominations, to aid ministers, churches and students for the ministry, and to coordinate charity hitherto undertaken sporadically and by individuals. A national initiative was then followed by imitative local schemes in various parts of the country.

At Bristol in June 1690 a meeting of ministers from Somerset, Gloucestershire, Wiltshire and Dorset subscribed to the *Essay of Accommodation*, which, together with the formation of the Common Fund, encouraged the United Ministers in and about London, formerly called Presbyterian and Congregational, to come together in March 1691 in the delightfully named Happy Union.

Matthew Mead, a Congregational minister, celebrated the Happy Union with a sermon on "The two sticks made one" (Ezekiel 37:15-18). Subsequently endorsed by associations of ministers in Devon, Hampshire, Cheshire, Lancashire and the West Riding of Yorkshire, it rested on the adoption of the *Heads of Agreement*. Under these the Presbyterians in effect agreed to discard a Presbyterian system of church government and to adopt the gathered church principle, while on their part the Congregationalists dropped the emphasis on some aspects of independency, e.g. their insistence on formal covenants and that ordination should be for just one congregation.

The designations Presbyterian and Independent (as Congregationalists were at first called) signify the division in the ranks of the Puritan clergy during the Commonwealth. Episcopacy, or governance of the Church by bishops, had been abolished and instead the Presbyterian clergy favored its rule by ministers and lay delegates from a number of parishes meeting together in classical presbyteries, which in turn sent their delegates to Regional and General assemblies. For a brief period such a scheme was partially introduced and the still extant Provincial Assembly of Lancashire and Cheshire is an indirect vestige of it. The Independents, however, held that each congregation ought to have autonomy in the conduct of its own affairs. Moreover, while the Independents generally favored taking this independence as far as separating from the State church, the Presbyterians preferred to remain within it, provided it was governed on Presbyterian lines. After the Act of Uniformity in 1662 the Presbyterians remained reluctant dissenters. Doctrinally, however, there was little between the parties. Both agreed that the Thirty-Nine Articles, The Westminster Confession (1643), The Savoy Revision of the Westminster Confession (1658), the Longer Catechism and the Shorter Catechism should determine what was acceptable.

The Happy Union unfortunately soon proved not to live up to its title. Beyond the *Heads of Agreement* other issues continued to divide, and within months the parties were quarrelling. Foremost was a disagreement over the kind of people who should be admitted to the ministry and the related problem of Antinomianism. The Presbyterians, favoring a regularly educated ministry, viewed with great concern the upstart "leather apron" preachers who occupied not a few Independent chapels, preaching an Antinomian message that, as human action could in no way affect whether a believer would or would not be saved, it was unnecessary for believers to obey the moral law.

With the shattering of theological consensus, Presbyterian divines were deprived of the opportunity to deliver the mid-week lecture at the

Congregationalists' Pinners' Hall meetinghouse, and in 1694 began their own a rival lecture on the same day in the Salters' Hall.

Added to this, a year earlier the Congregationalists formed their own Fund, leaving the Common Fund to the Presbyterians, who subsequently renamed it the Presbyterian Fund. Henceforth, the Presbyterian Fund supported ministers of moderate orthodoxy while the Congregational Fund maintained those of more radical Calvinistic views. Such was the theological alignment of the two major Dissenting parties at the end of the seventeenth century, each supported by its separate Fund. It is one of the more curious and confusing aspects of the history of English Protestant Dissent that by the end of the eighteenth century these two positions had been reversed, with English Presbyterians standing for latitude and the Congregationalists for rigid orthodoxy.

11

Beginnings of the Arian Movement

While Dissenters were occupied with matters of funding, chapel building, and ministerial recognition on the one hand, and the doctrinal questions of Predestination and Antinomianism on the other, it was amongst Anglicans that questions and doubts concerning the Trinity began to resurface at the beginning of the eighteenth century.

The first to attract attention was Thomas Emlyn, the minister of a dissenting congregation at Dublin, though an Anglican by upbringing. When it was noticed that Emlyn never preached about the Trinity, he responded by setting out his views in *An Humble Inquiry into the Scripture-Account of Jesus Christ* (1702). As a result he was put on trial in 1703, convicted and sentenced to a year's imprisonment, plus a fine of £1,000. Unable to pay, his incarceration was extended to two years before he was allowed to return to London.

In 1710 William Whiston, who had succeeded Sir Isaac Newton (himself a closet anti-Trinitarian) as the Lucasian Professor of Mathematics at Cambridge, was deprived of his chair for Arianism, the belief that Christ was not coequal with God, but subordinate to the Father and not pre-existent.

Two years later, in 1712, Dr. Samuel Clarke, rector of St James's Piccadilly, London, published *The Scripture-Doctrine of the Trinity,* citing no less than 1,251 passages to prove God the Father was supreme and Christ and the Holy Spirit only subordinate,

Dr. Samuel Clarke

which he held was the true interpretation of the threefold terminology found in the New Testament.

Clarke also made a revision of the *Book of Common Prayer* from which he omitted the Athanasian Creed and the Trinitarian formulas. This was to form the basis of the revised Anglican liturgy used by Theophilus Lindsey when he opened Essex Street Chapel in 1774, the first avowedly Unitarian place of worship, to which he hoped to attract disaffected Anglicans rather than Dissenters. It also partly explains the liturgical traditions that were a feature of not a few Unitarian churches up to the 1960s, culminating in *Orders of Worship*, of which rarely used sets can still be found in chapel vestry cupboards.

The Salters' Hall Controversy

Although it was from an Anglican source, the publication of *The Scripture-Doctrine of the Trinity* did not pass unnoticed by Dissenters. A year later James Pierce, a Presbyterian minister at Exeter, who had known Whiston and read Clarke, was denounced for having persuaded a student at Joseph Hallett's academy that scripture supported Arianism. To satisfy the objectors Pierce was asked to preach a sermon on the Trinity, but it is said he so rushed the crucial part that the heresy hunters were left with insufficient notes on which to base accusations.

The Exeter Assembly of Divines then called upon its members throughout Devon and Cornwall to submit their views on the doctrine. The returns were regarded as unsatisfactory, not least because three out of the four Presbyterian ministers in Exeter itself, including Pierce and Hallett, proved to hold Arian opinions. Pierce's own response maintained that though the Son and the Holy Ghost were divine persons, they were subordinate to God the Father.

The failure of the Divines to resolve the differences led a committee of Exeter's Presbyterian laymen to resort to the custom of seeking guidance from the dissenting ministers in London. To determine what advice they should send back to Exeter, the Presbyterian, Independent and Baptist ministers of the City met at Salters' Hall on two days in February 1719. Their decision, by 57 votes to 53, was to refuse to formulate any compositions or interpretations of the Trinity. It was tantamount to saying: you have the Bible, what more do you want? If the issue that caused the Salters' Hall controversy was the Trinity, the outcome was a refusal to make articles of belief a test of faith.

The controversy at Salters' Hall, 1719. A contemporary satirical print.
The Subscribers are in the balcony, saying, "All you that are for the
Trinity come up. We have subscribed." The Non-Subscribers are on the
ground floor, saying, "We will have no impositions."

Meanwhile, in the South West, events were moving apace. Before the reply from London was on its way, the Presbyterian meeting houses at Exeter had closed their doors to Arians, leaving Hallett and Pierce with no other course than to begin a new congregation, the Mint Meeting.

A month after the Salters' Hall meeting, in March 1719, at another meeting in Salters' Hall, the defeated minority of London ministers subscribed to a Trinitarian declaration. This was to create a lasting distinction amongst Dissenters, between "subscribers," who required assent to creedal formulas as a test of faith, and "non-subscribers," who would not be bound by them. The subscribers were mostly Congregationalists and Particular Baptists remaining loyal to Calvinism, with its rigid doctrine of Predestination whereby only the elect would be saved. The non-subscribers in the main were Presbyterians and General Baptists. While few of them at this stage had gone as far as Arianism, they nonetheless had an aversion to what they saw as human creeds.

After the Salters' Hall controversy, Calvinism, which restricted salvation to the elect, gradually gave way to a more humane Arminianism, with the possibility of salvation being open to all who would receive the free grace of God in Christ. Throughout the remainder of the eighteenth century, the non-subscribing Dissenters and General Baptists moved gradually through Arminianism to Arianism, and from Arianism to Socinianism. It was, however, only after 1730 that Arian views began to emerge, while Socinian or outright Unitarian opinions were rarely heard amongst Dissenters before the 1790s. It would be early in the nineteenth century before they could openly call themselves Unitarians if they wished to do so; even then some did not, preferring to emphasize their Non-Subscription rather than defining their Christology.

The Emergence of Unitarianism in Specific Congregations

In local Dissenting congregations the changes took time. Arian ministers were in time succeeded by others holding that worship and prayer should be addressed to God alone. The transitions did not, however, go uncontested and there are numerous examples of congregations where a section of the worshippers seceded to form an Independent chapel where Calvinism could still be upheld. Today the legacy of these divisions can be seen where a United Reformed church (formerly Congregational) is situated within a short distance of a Unitarian chapel, each with a history in common up to circa 1790. Moreover, the processes were hardly democratic since a few liberal trustees could keep an Arian minister in place against the wishes of the orthodox majority of the congregation. Arguably, fewer of the old meetinghouses would now be in Unitarian hands if decisions had been made democratically.

The Dissenting Academies

The dissenting academies, where ministers were trained, also proved to be fertile ground for the development of Arian and, later, Unitarian views. They were founded in the late seventeenth century to provide higher education for Nonconformists who were excluded from the ancient universities in England by the Test Acts, which required entrants to be communicating members of the Church of England. A few Dissenters enrolled for all or part of their education at universities in Scotland or the Netherlands, where tests did not apply, but the majority of those preparing for the ministry, medicine, law or commerce attended one of the twenty-three or so academies run by scholarly ministers in locations where they were also pastor of a congregation.

The full story of these remarkable institutions and their place in the development of English higher education is recorded in H. McLachlan, *English Education Under the Test Acts*. McLachlan's claim that they provided an education superior to any in the English universities at that time has recently been disputed, but the classically based curriculum of the universities had certainly failed to keep pace with the deluge of new learning. In contrast, the academies were adaptable and innovative, introducing modern languages, science and applied mathematics.

At the Northampton academy run by Philip Doddridge between 1729 and 1751, the teaching was in English rather than Latin. The course took four years to complete and the subjects included ancient languages, literature, anatomy, history, geography, metaphysics, geometry, algebra, trigonometry, conic sections, celestial mechanics, rhetoric, logic, natural and experimental philosophy, physics, astronomy, as well as divinity. Here, as in the academies generally, the primary purpose of studying the sciences was to deduce arguments in favor of the wisdom and benevolence of God.

The experimental and critical methods of the new learning, so useful to the advancement of science and technology, also proved a challenge to existing standards of theological orthodoxy. At Samuel Jones's academy in Gloucester, in 1711, the students studied John Locke's *Essay Concerning Human Understanding*, in which they met the claim that knowledge is derived from experience and revelation has to be judged by reason. When applied to religion, these ideas opened up for exploration realms of thought that had hitherto been forbidden territory, and propositions formerly condemned as heresy.

Not confined to candidates for the ministry, academies also admitted students for the other learned professions and for commerce and industry. In 1745 John Wilkinson, the greatest of the eighteenth-century iron-masters (and Joseph Priestley's brother-in-law), was a student at Caleb Rotheram's academy in Kendal, Westmoreland. Of the 300 students educated under Richard Frankland at Rathmell academy, near Settle, Yorkshire, only a third became ministers. They would, however, play a prominent role in the development of liberal Nonconformity, not least in their control of its financial resources as trustees of the Funds they created. Ministers were not, and generally still are not, appointed as trustees, because under charity law this would make them ineligible to receive any benefit from the funds.

Some academies remained strictly orthodox and continued to train ministers for Independent and Baptist congregations, but the liberal ones where students were funded by grants from the Presbyterian Fund were the breeding grounds for Arian, Socinian and proto-Unitarian views, which would further drive the wedge between Subscribers and Non-Subscribers, making it necessary for them to be differentiated as Evangelical and Rational Dissenters.

The general decline of the academies at the end of the eighteenth century, and the closure of the academy at Warrington, Cheshire, in 1786, led to the foundation of Manchester Academy in Manchester that year, and in its subsequent locations at York, 1803-1840, Manchester again, 1840-1853, London, 1853-1889, and finally in Oxford. Under the successive names of Manchester Academy; Manchester College, York; Manchester New College, London; Manchester College, Oxford; and Harris Manchester College, Oxford, it has continued up to the present day to provide ministers for the Unitarian and Free Christian churches.

A chronology for the eighteenth-century progress from orthodoxy, through Arianism to Socinianism/Unitarianism, is suggested by the fact that in 1761, when Joseph Priestley took up his post as tutor at Warrington academy, all three of his academic colleagues were still Arians. He also remarked of the other ministers in the area, that "only Mr. Seddon of Manchester was a Socinian." In due course Priestley himself would adopt first the term Socinian, then Unitarian. In the 1790s he was joined by a spate of other dissenting ministers preaching Unitarian opinions. Not until the repeal of the Trinity Act in 1813 could they do so without fear of the legal penalties.

College Fold, Rathmell, near Settle, Yorkshire,
where Richard Frankland opened his Academy in 1670

12

"Humanitarian" Unitarianism

Unitarian opinions could not legally be expressed before the repeal of the Trinity Act in 1813, but in the fourth quarter of the eighteenth century there were some, in both Dissent and the Established Church, who were prepared to go beyond Arianism to what was then referred to as "Humanitarian" Unitarianism.

Eighteenth-century Arians had been Unitarian insofar as they asserted that God the Father is supreme and that Jesus is subordinate and of a different substance, but they had nonetheless attributed to Jesus a semi-divine nature. The new "Humanitarian" Unitarians went further in regarding Jesus as essentially human. Unfortunately, such a view is open to misrepresentation by detractors, for this was not to suggest he was merely like other men, or to underestimate his exemplary life as a model for humanity.

Amongst the "Humanitarians," Caleb Fleming (1698-1779), minister at Pinners' Hall and probably an Independent rather than a Presbyterian, as the Pinners' Hall congregation was associated with the Congregationalists, is said to have been the first Dissenting minister to preach a humanitarian doctrine of Christ throughout his entire ministry. In the confession of faith at his ordination he affirmed that the New Testament contains a revelation worthy of God to give and man to receive, and promised to preach as he "should from time to time understand it."

Nathaniel Lardner (1684-1768), another Independent, was even more significant. Never ordained, he was averse to anything resembling a theological test, passing from Trinitarianism to Arianism, and finally to humanitarian Unitarianism. His opinion, that "There is one God, even the Father; Christ is a man with a reasonable soul and human body, especially favored by God," was made explicit in his *Letter on the Logos*, which persuaded Joseph Priestley to adopt Unitarianism.

*Nathaniel Lardner
His Letter on the Logos
persuaded Joseph Priestley to
adopt Unitarianism.*

Paul Cardale of Oat Street Chapel, Evesham, Worcestershire, published his *True Doctrine of the New Testament concerning Jesus Christ* in 1767, which was influential in encouraging the spread of Unitarian views in the Midlands.

Further north, John Seddon, the minister at Cross Street Chapel, Manchester, was referred to in 1761 as a Socinian, though his successors at Cross Street returned to Arianism and were slow to advance beyond it, leaving it to a new congregation at Mosley Street to be in the vanguard of theological change. Seddon was a pioneer of the historical investigation of Christian doctrine.

The advocates of humanitarian Unitarianism were geographically widespread in London, the Midlands and the north of England, which suggests its pervasive character in mid eighteenth- century Britain, but it was late in the century before it gathered force.

Joseph Priestley

Joseph Priestley developed these ideas to become the first really eminent Unitarian. He gave the movement (if it can be called one at this stage) strength and coherence. Now chiefly remembered for discoveries in chemistry and electricity, he regarded his primary calling as that of a dissenting minister and theologian.

Born at Fieldhead, near Leeds, in March 1733, Priestley's background was Calvinist. Brought up by a pious aunt, he was barred from his local Independent congregation because of doubts concerning original sin. After his early education at Batley Grammar School he entered the dissenting academy at Daventry, where under liberal influences he abandoned any remaining traces of Calvinism, though his brother Timothy was always to remain an orthodox Independent minister. Completing his course in 1755, Priestley became minister at Needham Market, Suffolk, where his *Scripture Doctrine of Remission* denying the atonement and Trinity was published.

Dr. Joseph Priestley
A commemorative medal struck by J. G. Hancock

In 1758 he moved to Nantwich, Cheshire, where a speech impediment continued to inhibit his pulpit oratory to such an extent that he advised the congregation that he would concentrate on running his school.

Priestley's appointment as tutor in languages and classics at Warrington academy in 1761 offered greater security than he could ever expect from the rural congregations. He now set aside speculative theology and engaged in duties that would give him an academic and national reputation. Publication of his *Compilation of Eminent Men* led to the conferment of the degree of Doctor of Laws at Edinburgh in 1764, and his *History of Electricity* secured his admission as a Fellow of the Royal Society in 1766. Yet the fact that he sought ordination and continued to preach occasionally suggests he may have foreseen a need to return to pastoral ministry, a circumstance which presented itself when he resigned from Warrington, partly on account of his wife's poor health and partly because of difficulties which eventually led to the academy's closure.

Mill Hill Chapel, Leeds, appointed him as its minister in 1766. His theological position at this point was not yet openly Socinian. Five years earlier at Warrington he had remarked on Seddon's Socinianism, as if he had not yet settled the Christological question. A return to pastoral ministry not only afforded, but also required the renewal of his attention to speculative theology, when he read Nathaniel Lardner's *Letter on the Logos*. Later, he wrote: "I became a Socinian soon after my settlement at Leeds; and after giving closest attention to the subject, I have seen more and more reason to be satisfied with that opinion to this day, and likewise to be more impressed with the idea of its importance."

Theologically and philosophically, Priestley and his supporters were Determinists, Necessarians and Materialists. Determinism is the thesis that any event whatsoever is an instance of some law of nature; similarly, necessarianism is the thesis that actions are determined by prior history; and materialism is the thesis that everything is wholly dependent on matter for its existence and, more specifically, that there is only one fundamental kind of reality and this is material, and that human beings and other living creatures are not dual beings composed of a material body and an immaterial soul, but are fundamentally bodily in nature.

Some scientific work was continued alongside Priestley's pastoral duties in Leeds, including experiments on "fixed air" (carbon dioxide) and carbonated water, for which he was awarded the Copley Medal of the Royal Society in 1773. The experiments were later continued after he

Warrington Academy

Joseph Priestley, satirically portrayed in 1791 as
"Doctor Phlogiston, the PRIESTLEY politican or the political priest!"

left Leeds to become secretary and literary companion to Lord Shelburne, who would serve briefly as Prime Minister of the United Kingdom in 1782-83. Shelburne provided Priestley with generous study and laboratory facilities. In August 1774, Priestley discovered oxygen, or what he called "dephlogisticated air." It was while traveling with Shelburne in France that he later met Lavoisier, the other contender to the claim. Priestley's friendship with Shelburne had arisen from their shared support for the American colonists in their declaration of independence, but differences between them later led to the termination of the patronage.

Thrown back on his own resources, Priestley settled at Birmingham, mainly because his brother-in-law John Wilkinson, the ironmaster, provided a house for him. As a result he became co-minister of the New Meeting, where he completed two major works in his scientific and theological fields: *Different Kinds of Airs* and *The History of the Corruptions of Christianity*. Leisure at Birmingham afforded the company of his friends in the Lunar Society, which has been so well treated in Jenny Uglow's *The Lunar Men*.

Yet if life was moderately comfortable, it was at this period that he attracted increasing opposition from Church and King mobs for his sympathies with the French Revolution. It led to the sacking of his house and laboratory on 14 July 1791, the eve of the Revolution Society dinner to celebrate the anniversary of the storming of the Bastille. Seeking refuge, the Priestleys went by way of Worcester to Hackney, London, where he succeeded Richard Price as minister at Gravel-Pit Chapel and lectured at Hackney College.

The College, however, was increasingly in financial difficulties as supporters withheld their subscriptions, fearful of the real or imagined Unitarian and republican radical opinions with which the students were being inculcated. England grew increasingly uncongenial and in April 1794 the Priestleys emigrated to America to join their son William at Northumberland, Pennsylvania, where he was partly responsible for the founding of a Unitarian society. Here Joseph Priestley died on 6 February 1804.

In the context of Unitarianism Priestley's religious and political ideas are much more significant than his science, though the latter should not be overlooked. In his own lifetime the work on electricity was regarded as more important than the chemistry. He also detected the photosynthesis by which plants restore the air, turning it from carbon dioxide to oxygen. At a humbler level he chanced upon the use of rubber as a pencil eraser.

Priestley's contribution to the Unitarian ethos may be summarized under three heads: Firstly, his theological transition from Calvinism to Unitarianism, stemming from his early questioning of original sin and the doctrine of the atonement; secondly, his gradual acceptance of critical methods in relation to the scriptures, first rejecting the virgin birth, while for a time still retaining belief in the miracles and the resurrection; and thirdly, his social and political radicalism coupled with support for civil and religious liberty. In the nineteenth century Thomas Belsham retained Priestley's Determinism, Necessarianism and Materialism, as at first did James Martineau, until he led the main body of Unitarians to abandon it in favor of a more intuitional style of faith. Priestley's stance would become the basis of scientific humanism.

Theophilus Lindsey

It was while Priestley was minister in Leeds, and becoming the leading promulgator of Unitarian opinion amongst Dissenters, that he became acquainted with Theophilus Lindsey, vicar of Catterick, Yorkshire, the son-in-law of Francis Blackburne, rector of Richmond and archdeacon of Cleveland. Blackburne and Lindsey were at this time prominent members of a group of Church of England clergy agitating for the relaxation of subscription to the Thirty-Nine Articles, which was required of clergy on taking up new appointments. Blackburne's other clergyman son-in-law, John Disney, would in due course succeed Lindsey as minister of Essex Street Chapel.

Lindsey and Priestley remained lifelong friends, constantly consulting each other about their opinions and publications. They were, however, different in several respects, not least of which was Lindsey's background in the Church of England.

Born at Middlewich, Cheshire, on 20 June 1723, Theophilus Lindsey was the son of a prosperous salt manufacturer with aristocratic connections. His godfather was the Earl of Huntingdon, the husband of Selina, founder of the Countess of Huntingdon's Connexion, and he became the protégé of Lady Betty and Lady Ann Hastings. Educated at Leeds Grammar School and St. John's College, Cambridge, he secured a fellowship in 1747, but in 1753 accepted the living of Kirkby Wiske, Yorkshire. There he married Hannah, Blackburne's daughter, before becoming rector of Piddletown, Dorset in 1756. Increasingly troubled regarding the doctrine of the Trinity and his subscription to the Thirty-Nine Articles, he compromised for a

Theophilus Lindsey, MA
Vicar of Catterick
Minister of the first avowedly Unitarian
church in Great Britain

time, returning to Yorkshire in 1763 as vicar of Catterick. During his ten years incumbency there he conducted an effective pastoral ministry, which because of his vigorous enthusiasm was identified by his parishioners as "methodism." It included the formation of a Sunday school, which may have been even earlier than Robert Raikes's experiment at Gloucester, generally regarded as the first.

Although the leadership of the agitation for the relaxation of subscription to the Thirty-Nine Articles came mainly from a group of clergy in Yorkshire, including Francis Blackburne of Richmond, Lindsey of Catterick and Christopher Wyvill of Constable Burton, it was organized nationally as the Feathers Tavern Association, taking its name from the inn on the Strand, London, where signatures for the petitioning of Parliament were collected. The outcome was a Bill which was debated in Parliament on 6 February 1772, and overwhelmingly defeated by 217 votes to 71.

The Feathers Tavern petition had secured considerable support, but on its defeat only about six clergymen resigned their livings or College fellowships. They included Thomas Fishe Palmer, later to be deported to Australia as one of the "Scottish Political Martyrs"; John Jebb, Fellow of Peterhouse, Cambridge; John Disney; Edward Evanston, Vicar of Tewkesbury; Gilbert Wakefield, who as a deacon left the Church without being ordained priest, and Theophilus Lindsey. Several of them explained the step they had taken as morally compelling. Samuel Clarke, on the other hand, failed to see or act on the inconsistency of his position with the Articles of the Church of England.

Refusing invitations to a number of places, including, it is said, a tutorship at Warrington Academy, Lindsey resigned the vicarage of Catterick in November 1773 and went to London. Obtaining premises in

Essex Street off the Strand, he began holding services in April 1774 for a congregation now regarded as having been the first avowedly Unitarian church in England. Essex Street Chapel was opened on 29 March 1778 with the primary intention of attracting disaffected members of the Church of England. To satisfy Anglican sensibilities, an adapted version of the *Book of Common Prayer Reformed According to the Plan of the Late Dr. Samuel Clarke* was used for worship.

Lindsey then published a defense of his action in *An Apology ... on resigning the Vicarage of Catterick*, in which he explained that the basis of his position was the inappropriateness of offering prayer and worship to Jesus, whom he regarded unequivocally as a human figure. Compared with Priestley, Lindsey was not a very profound thinker, but he left his mark on Unitarianism not only by his assertion that prayer and worship should be offered only to God the Father, but also by the courageous honesty of resigning the living of Catterick. He could not, of course, resign his Anglican orders, as this was impossible before the Clerical Disabilities Act of 1870.

After a little over a century, the depleted Essex Street congregation united in 1887 with the Kensington congregation established in 1867, to become Essex Church, Kensington. The old chapel site was developed as Essex Hall to accommodate the British and Foreign Unitarian Association's secretariat and subsequently, after 1928, also that of the General Assembly of Unitarian and Free Christian Churches. Destroyed by enemy action in 1944, the Hall was rebuilt and reopened on the same site in October 1958.

13

Becoming a Denomination

The revised Church of England liturgy used by Theophilus Lindsey for the worship at Essex Street Chapel proved to be unsuccessful in attracting the disaffected Anglicans he had hoped would share his non-Trinitarian views. Increasingly the chapel's support came from Dissenters. Hopes of sustaining the Anglican leadership failed when his brother-in-law and successor, John Disney, who had introduced an even more radically revised Prayer Book, inherited the estates of Thomas Brand Hollis and retired to the Essex countryside. Unable to find another Anglican, the congregation had no other option but to appoint a Dissenting minister.

Thomas Belsham

The choice fell upon Thomas Belsham, an Independent, who had become Unitarian while he was tutor at Daventry academy. Belsham became Lindsey's biographer with the publication of his *Memoirs of Theophilus Lindsey, MA*, 1812, and was largely responsible for the accelerated growth of Unitarianism during the early to mid-nineteenth century. Yet his significance as the great organizer of the movement has tended to be glossed over due to the calumnies he suffered during the party rivalries that were a feature of mid nineteenth-century developments.

While possibilities for advance were obviously limited before the repeal of the Trinity Act in 1813, there were some positive developments in the wake of the foundation of Essex Street Chapel. Lindsey himself had been responsible for another new congregation at Plymouth Dock, the naval dockyard, now Devonport. The chapel there made good progress until Rational Dissent became identified with support for the French Revolution, whereupon Commissioner Fanshawe of the dockyard refused to employ its members, with inevitable consequences for the

Thomas Belsham

rapid decline of the congregation. The meetinghouse has survived as the "Old Chapel" public house, with a gracious acknowledgement of its origins hanging in the vestibule.

Mosley Street, Manchester, was another congregation that emerged at this stage. It provided a forthright Unitarian alternative to the Arian theology to which Cross Street Chapel, a quarter of a mile away, had reverted after the Socinian ministry of John Seddon. Situated in the once fashionable but declining Georgian area of the city, it sold its premises to commercial interests in 1836 and moved to the leafy suburbs of Upper Brook Street, where Sir Charles Barry designed for it the first Nonconformist chapel to be built in the new Gothic style. It is rather strange that it adopted the title Upper Brook Street Free Church, eschewing the name "Unitarian," but this might have been the result of the challenges then being made to the ownership of Unitarian property by orthodox Dissenters.

Shrewsbury is an example of the influence that Lindsey's initiative also had on a few chapels with origins in the Old Dissent. It quickly adopted his revised Prayer Book style of worship and along with not a few other Unitarian chapels continued with its service book well into the 1960s. Though now almost a thing of the past, echoes of the set prayers from *Orders of Worship* (1932) are still occasionally heard in present-day worship.

When Belsham became Unitarian in 1789 there are said to have been only two avowedly Unitarian congregations in England, presumably those at Essex Street and Plymouth Dock. Yet by 1810 the number was 20, and by 1825 there were 200, plus 12 more in Scotland and 34 in Wales. Belsham's role was that of a successful administrator who creates a movement in the wake of an initial theological or spiritual impetus. He was to Lindsey what Demetrius Hunyadi had been to Francis Dávid in Transylvania, and Jabez Bunting to John Wesley for the growth of English Methodism.

Born of Independent, Calvinistic stock at Bedford in 1750, Belsham had studied at Daventry academy, where on completion of his course he remained as assistant tutor from 1771 to 1778. He removed to be minister at Worcester from 1778 to 1781, before returning to Daventry as minister and divinity tutor until 1789. Concentrating his teaching in support of the orthodox case in the Unitarian controversy, he found himself increasingly being persuaded in favor of Unitarianism. Successively Arian, Socinian and eventually Unitarian, in 1789 he resigned from Daventry and was persuaded by Priestley and Lindsey to take on the oversight of Hackney College, which was established in 1786 with the purpose of training dissenting ministers to make good the shortfall in numbers caused by recent closures, for various reasons, of the academies at Exeter, Hoxton and Warrington.

At this stage there was none of the advance that Unitarianism would make under Belsham's role as its leading nineteenth-century propagandist. Indeed, Belsham and his fellow tutors, including the biblical scholar and religious controversialist Gilbert Wakefield, were so pessimistic about any future for organized religion that several of their students, including the writer, critic and painter William Hazlitt, abandoned the idea of entering the ministry.

In spite of his pessimism in the wake of the problems at Hackney, as early as 1791 Belsham was instrumental in starting the Unitarian Book Society, whose full title was The Society for Promoting Christian Knowledge and the Practice of Virtue by the Distribution of Books. This was the first of several organizations that were to pave the way for the development of a Unitarian denomination.

The failure of the college in 1796 released Belsham to succeed Disney at Essex Street. There he remained for twenty years, engaged in the scholarly activity, which prepared him for the organizational role he would later play. In 1811 he published *A Calm Inquiry into the Scripture Doctrine concerning the Person of Christ*. He was also a pioneer of Biblical criticism. His *Improved Version of the New Testament* of 1808 led the way for an agitation for the revision of the Authorized Version, and in a sermon for the Provincial Assembly held at Warrington in August 1821 he declared Genesis to be incompatible with science.

Belsham's *Memoirs of Theophilus Lindsey*, in addition to providing a biography of the founder of England's first avowedly Unitarian chapel, also had unexpected and remarkable repercussions for developments in the United States. An appended letter by William Wells, on "The State of Unitarianism in New England," caused a chain of events which led to William Ellery Channing delivering a sermon on "Unitarian Christianity" at an ordination at Baltimore in 1819, in which for the first time he openly identified his New England liberal Christianity with Unitarianism.

Today, Belsham is scarcely remembered. This is difficult to explain, though there are some signs that he was the victim of deliberate vilification by those who favored an emphasis on what they regarded to be the catholicity of the old English Presbyterianism, rather that the more strident sectarian Unitarianism which Belsham represented and under whose leadership it was to make remarkable headway during the early nineteenth century. His obscurity may also partly result from the ridicule to which he was often subjected because of his rotund figure. An amusing, if unkind, anecdote survives at Chowbent Chapel, Atherton, Lancashire, where an alteration to wood paneling is said to be the result of a carpenter having to be summoned to extract him from the impressive three-deck pulpit.

Robert Aspland

Belsham's leadership of the emergent denomination passed to Robert Aspland, who has been called the father of organized Unitarianism in Great Britain. Born in 1782 to a Baptist shopkeeper at Wicken, Cambridgeshire, Aspland went for his initial ministerial training at Battersea, South London, before proceeding to Bristol Academy in 1799, and thence to Marischal College in the University of Aberdeen, where he first began to doubt the Calvinism of orthodox Baptists and left the University. For a while he gave up the idea of a ministerial career, but he was persuaded to accept an invitation from the General Baptist Chapel at Newport, Isle of Wight, one of the General Baptist congregations whose

Robert Aspland

theology at that time was becoming increasingly Unitarian. From there, in 1805, he succeeded Belsham as minister of Gravel-Pit Chapel, Hackney.

This leading Unitarian pulpit provided Aspland with the base from which to begin his lifelong task of creating the organizational structures of a Unitarian denomination. Starting in 1806 with a failing periodical, he turned it into the *Monthly Repository*, a serious forum for theology and biblical criticism, which reported Unitarian events and gave scattered congregations a sense of their importance and national cohesion. Later, when the *Repository* became a literary journal of distinction under W. J. Fox, Aspland continued to deploy his journalist's skills for a more popular readership in the *Christian Reformer*, which he founded in 1815.

In 1812 Aspland established a new Unitarian academy at Durham House, Hackney, to train men as popular Unitarian preachers, but, due to ill health and financial problems, he was forced to abandon it in 1818. Most importantly, in 1806 he led the movement to establish the Unitarian Fund to support the missionary work of Richard Wright, and became its first secretary. Later, in 1825, he played a key role in the foundation of the British and Foreign Unitarian Association, of which he was twice secretary, 1825-30 and 1835-41.

14

Spreading the Message

The main vehicle for Unitarian advance at the beginning of the nineteenth century was the Unitarian Fund for Promoting Unitarianism by means of Popular Preaching, founded by Robert Aspland in 1806. Its purpose was to provide financial support for ministers and congregations, to make grants for buildings or special efforts, and to promote missionary endeavor, which it did mainly through the campaigns of Richard Wright. It also encouraged the formation of local Fellowship Funds, whereby wealthy congregations made donations for needy causes and concerns elsewhere, and it fostered contacts with kindred movements abroad, particularly the Unitarian churches in Transylvania, newly rediscovered by the British churches in the 1820s. The Fund favored the deployment of popular preaching techniques, more appealing to the emotions than had generally been the custom amongst Rational Dissenters. It was a tendency that met with some resistance. Belsham himself was initially doubtful, though he eventually became its great supporter. This did not, however, prevent polemical preaching in which Unitarian doctrine was forthrightly promoted.

Richard Wright

Richard Wright was appointed the Unitarian Fund's missionary at its foundation and remained in the post until he returned to the regular ministry in 1822, with the Unitarian Baptist congregation at Trowbridge, Wiltshire. Born at Blakeney, Norfolk, Wright's family had Anglican connections, but they became actively involved with a strict Calvinist independent congregation where Richard became a lay preacher at an early age. When his Arminian opinions led to his expulsion from this group he was for a while a preacher with the Methodists, until he joined the Johnsonian Baptists,

Richard Wright
First missionary of the Unitarian Fund

named after John Johnson of Eccles, who led a small group of dissident
Baptist congregations situated mainly in East Anglia. As pastor of their
congregation at Wisbech, Cambridgeshire, he adopted Unitarianism and
henceforth became the zealous apostle of its new aggressive, propagandist
wing. As the Fund's missionary, Wright journeyed the length and breadth
of the country, mostly on foot, averaging 2,000 miles per annum, taking
the Unitarian doctrine to villages where no churches existed. Finally, in
1827, he sought obscurity as minister to the small isolated congregation
at Kirkstead, Lincolnshire, where he died in 1836.

While some were now concerned with aggressive Unitarian propaganda, others were actively engaged in agitations for the repeal of the
disabling Acts, which limited the scope of Nonconformity generally and
Unitarianism in particular. Political opinions which had to be suppressed
during the war with France, to avoid accusations of sedition, could again
be openly expressed after the victory at Waterloo in 1815. There was a
revival of Reform movements to repeal the Test and Corporation Acts,
which eventually succeeded in 1828, followed by Catholic Emancipation
the following year. Repeal of the Trinity Act in 1813 had brought some
relief in making it possible to openly express Unitarian views without fear

of punitive consequences, but the other disabilities remained and would not be entirely eliminated until 1880 when, at the end of a mopping up of the other disabling measures, dissenters finally secured the right to be buried in parish churchyards without Anglican rites.

Among Unitarians this renewed agitation was given organizational form in 1819 by the formation of the Association for the Protection and Extension of the Civil Rights of Unitarians, generally known as the Civil Rights Association.

The British and Foreign Unitarian Association

The overlapping functions of the Book Society, the Unitarian Fund and the Civil Rights Association led to a movement for their amalgamation. First the Unitarian Fund and the Civil Rights Association agreed to a merger. They were joined the following year by the Book Society to form the British and Foreign Unitarian Association. By the strangest of coincidences its inaugural meeting was held on 26 May 1825, the very same day as that of the American Unitarian Association in Boston.

The British and Foreign Unitarian Association had four classes of membership: District Associations, Congregations and Fellowship Funds, Individual and Honorary members. The initial success was not sustained, partly due to the emergence of two divergent strains within Unitarianism: the one zealous for the advance of Unitarianism on doctrinal lines and the other holding to the hope of a more broadly based liberal church eschewing the use of the name Unitarian in the titles of the chapels. The latter view, favored by James Martineau, led to the steady decline of congregational support for the new body. Moreover, in the effort to save Unitarian chapels from the threat they were beginning to face at this stage from orthodox Dissenters wishing to reclaim them, the term "English Presbyterianism" was increasingly adopted in preference to anything overtly Unitarian. None-theless, apart from the triennial meeting of the National Conference, the British and Foreign Unitarian Association remained the principal feature of a developing Unitarian denominationalism.

The inclusion of "Foreign" in the title of the British and Foreign Uni-tarian Association must have been prophetic or anticipatory at this stage, rather than real. It did, however, aid the Rev. Israel Worsley's attempt to establish a Unitarian chapel in Paris in 1831, which was attended by British, American and German expatriates, but which failed when they fled the cholera epidemic in 1832. It is true that Transylvanian Unitarians had recently been discovered, but beyond a friendly correspondence it could never have been imagined that the Association would ever constitutionally encompass such an ancient and established foreign Unitarian Church. Emigration on any scale was barely under way by this time. In the 1820s there were only 216,000 movements of citizen passengers to and from United Kingdom ports, compared with 1,495,000 in the 1840s, when Unitarian emigrants settling in Canada planted churches at Montreal (1842) and Toronto (1845). In the 1850s Unitarian churches were established in Australia: Sydney (1850), Melbourne (1852) and Adelaide (1855). A Unitarian Society founded at Auckland in New Zealand, circa 1861, had a short-lived existence until 1866. It was re-established in 1898, and erected a church building in 1901.

In Canada, a Post Office Mission, founded in 1870 and run by the Montreal and Toronto Unitarians, did much to extend the movement. In the 1890s, Icelandic immigrants began holding services that led to the formation of the First Icelandic Unitarian Church of Winnipeg in 1891, and in 1909 a congregation was launched at Vancouver. This gradual extension accelerated after World War II. Postwar decline of colonialism resulted in the lessening of the Canadians' ties with the British General Assembly and an increase of cooperation with the American Unitarian Association. In 1961, the same year that Unitarians and Universalists in the United States combined to form the Unitarian Universalist Association (UUA), the Canadian Unitarian Council-Conseil Unitarien du Canada (CUC) was formed "within the framework of the continental Unitarian Universalist Association." Since 2002, the CUC has been independent of the UUA, though the two organizations have continued to cooperate in the areas of youth programming and ministerial settlement.

General Baptists, Methodist Unitarians and the Christian Brethren

Unitarianism in Britain was further advanced in the late eighteenth and early to mid-nineteenth centuries by the accession of three small denominations, which had originated in secessions from orthodox connexions. First, the General Baptists gradually became doctrinally Unitarian from circa 1700. Then two small Methodist bodies, one a secession from the Wesleyan Methodist Connexion and the other from the Methodist New Connexion, were merged with, or absorbed into, the old English Presbyterian tradition.

Within the Baptist movement the General Baptists had always represented a liberal tradition of those who believed that salvation was generally
open to all, in contrast to the Particular Baptists who saw it as confined
particularly to the elect. In 1770, however, a group of the more doctrinally orthodox congregations withdrew to form what became known as
the New Connexion of General Baptists, leaving the liberals, who were
now referred to as the old General Baptists, free to develop doctrinally
along Unitarian lines. By 1815 several General Baptist congregations
had become formally associated with the Unitarian movement, though
they continued, as they still do, to unite in a General Baptist Assembly.
The churches were located mainly in areas of historic Baptist strength,
in Wiltshire, the South West and South Wales, and in Kent and Sussex.
Richard Wright's background was in this body, which was vigorous in the
propagation of Unitarian doctrine and contrasted markedly with the more
staid, non-proselytizing characteristics of the English Presbyterians. About
the same time, David Eaton, a Baptist layman in York, also discovered
Unitarianism and believed that instead of remaining on the defensive, as
Unitarians had been at the time of the Trinity Act, they should become
more aggressively propagandist.

The Baptist split had occurred partly because William Vidler, who had
adopted Universalist views under the influence of the American Elhanan
Winchester, had joined their Assembly. Vidler, who had met Richard
Wright, also adopted Unitarianism, taking the General Baptists with him
in that direction. It has been suggested that this caused Universalism to
be eclipsed as a separate movement in Great Britain. However, a more
general reason for the failure of Universalism to make headway in Britain,
compared with its growth as a large denomination in America, might have
been the success of Methodism, which, with its Arminian doctrine of
grace, obviated some of the need for the broader opportunity of salvation
offered by Universalism.

The Methodist Unitarian Movement was a small group of churches in
northeast Lancashire. Centered on Rochdale, with strong congregations
at Newchurch-in-Rossendale, Padiham and Todmorden, it was a product
of secession from the Wesleyan Methodist Connexion in 1806. That year,
Joseph Cooke, a Rochdale minister, had been expelled by the Methodist
Conference for denying that it was necessary to "feel" the assurance of
pardon for the forgiveness of sins. Sometimes referred to as Cookites, the
reluctance of Methodist Unitarians to accept feelings and emotions as nec-

Joseph Cooke
Leader of the Methodist Unitarians

essary evidence of true religion, coupled with their spirit of rational enquiry, gave them an affinity with the rational dissenting tradition of the English Presbyterians. They differed, however, from the mainstream Unitarian constituency in two respects: their church polity was connexional (not independent), and they were of a different socio-economic class. The members of their chapels were weavers, warpers, wool-sorters, over-lookers, hatters, cloggers and shoemakers, who sought redress for their economic oppression in the radical reform movements of the day: Political Reform Unions, Owenite Socialism and Chartism. They also played an important part in the formation of the Rochdale Pioneers' Equitable Co-operative Society in 1844, which, while it was not the first cooperative society, was the first to succeed. Their Clover Street Chapel in Rochdale was known locally as the "Co-op Chapel." Until 1844, when they became part of the general Unitarian denomination, they had a separate connexional identity. Their history and significance is recorded in H. McLachlan, *The Methodist Unitarian Movement* (Manchester, 1919).

The Christian Brethren Movement also developed from Methodist secession. In 1841 a Mossley minister, Joseph Barker, was expelled from the Methodist New Connexion for his rejection of the doctrine of original sin. As a result the Methodist New Connexion lost some 29 churches and 4,348 members, and though not all became Unitarian, many of them did. The movement was geographically widespread, with congregations as far afield as Newcastle-on-Tyne and Plymouth, but it was particularly strong in the Staffordshire Potteries, where Barker ministered after he left Mossley. Closer ties with the Unitarian movement seem to have developed when the Barkerites, as they were known, abandoned their original objection to a hired ministry. John Relly Beard, the founder and first principal of the Unitarian Home Missionary Board in 1854, declared that there was "an existing and growing demand for Unitarian ministers in churches among the Christian Brethren and other liberal and popular bodies." Barker eventually abandoned the churches to plunge himself into support for Chartism, but not before his press at Wortley, near Leeds, had published and distributed 30,000 copies of *Channing's Works*. The movement is fully explained in "The Christian Brethren Movement" in H. McLachlan, *A Nonconformist Library* (Manchester, 1923).

At the beginning of the nineteenth century, British Unitarianism was essentially a combination of the Rational Dissenting tradition and the modified Anglicanism of Lindsey. At the end, it had been radically altered by the influx of popular religious bodies with adherents who were less hidebound by polite society and who brought with them the missionary zeal of the Methodist connexions from which they had originally seceded. Thus, although the Evangelical Revival had been resisted by Rational Dissent and largely passed it by, some of its enthusiasm found a way into Unitarianism by these routes.

15

Nineteenth-Century Advance

The repeal of the Trinity Act in 1813 did not sanction Unitarian beliefs, but it relieved those holding them of the legal penalties. It was therefore a significant factor in the spread and increasing prosperity of Unitarianism during the early nineteenth century. The accession of the General Baptists, the Methodist Unitarians and the Christian Brethren, and the development of missionary activity all helped to increase the number of congregations. When the Religious Census was taken in 1851 there were 229 Unitarian places of worship in England and Wales, providing 68,554 sittings, plus 5 in Scotland with a further 1,950 sittings. Unitarian chapels for that day, 30 March 1851, returned attendances of 26,612 at morning services, 8,610 in the afternoons and 12,406 in the evenings, a total of 47,628.

This welcome progress was not however without some unfortunate negative consequences. The new freedom to be openly Unitarian was deeply resented by orthodox denominations and provoked active opposition. The opposition came chiefly from the Independents, now more commonly known as Congregationalists, and was focused in their attempts to regain control of old established chapels and trusts. They argued that these were being used for purposes contrary to the beliefs of their founders and for doctrines that were illegal at the time of their foundation. The Unitarians maintained, to the contrary, that the Open Trusts had permitted the gradual development of doctrinal opinion from Trinitarianism, through Arianism, to Unitarianism.

A Setback: The Wolverhampton Chapel and Lady Hewley Cases

The first legal challenge to Unitarian property came in 1817 when Congregationalists in Wolverhampton, Worcestershire, led by paint manufacturer Benjamin Mander, sought to obtain use of the town's Unitarian chapel. The case went through three trials and was eventually overtaken by the

Lady Hewley Trust litigation, judgment being reserved until the latter case was finally settled by the passage of the Dissenters' Chapels Act in 1844. By this time the costs of the case had exceeded the value of the Chapel and the judge ordered it to be sold. No purchaser could be found, except the Church of England, and in 1862 it somewhat ironically became an Anglican chapel of ease.

Further north, controversies over rightful ownership got properly under way with a speech in Manchester in 1824, when George Hadfield on behalf of the Congregationalists made a claim to a large number of places of worship held by the Unitarians, which it was argued should rightly belong to them. The case was well documented and published as *The Manchester Socinian Controversy* (1825), which, though compiled by detractors, provides a useful source of early chapel histories, provided the reader recognizes the bias against the Unitarians.

Wrangles over property were also accompanied by disputes about the application of trust funds and, a decade later, culminated in the Lady Hewley Case. The Lady Hewley Trust was associated with St Saviourgate Chapel, York, where doctrine, as was the case with many other Presbyterian dissenting chapels, had gradually become Unitarian by the early nineteenth century. Although the Trust made grants to Protestant Dissenting ministers irrespective of denominational affiliation, Unitarians were well represented amongst the trustees. In 1833, however, and again in 1836, the courts ruled that the Unitarian trustees should be removed and in future grants only made to ministers of orthodox chapels. Upheld by the House of Lords in 1842, the ruling caused great consternation, for if taken as a precedent it would result in the loss of all the older chapels and trusts.

The Dissenters' Chapels Act, 1844

With the Lady Hewley Case still unsettled and seemingly going against them, no year was bleaker than 1842 for nineteenth-century Unitarians. In defense, the British and Foreign Unitarian Association as if to stress the continuity with seventeenth and eighteenth-century English Presbyterianism, founded a "Presbyterian Union." It soon became apparent, however, that there was public sympathy for the plight of Unitarians. The Dissenters' Chapels Bill, drafted by the Unitarian lawyer Edwin Wilkins Field and promoted in the Commons by George William Wood, the member for Kendal, passed both Houses of Parliament with the support of W. E. Gladstone, and was given the Royal Assent in July 1844.

The measure finally settled the ownership of the disputed properties and safeguarded the old dissenting meeting houses and other Open Trust foundations, where it could be shown there was a continuous history of at least twenty-five years of Unitarian faith and practice. The newer congregations, specifically founded as Unitarian chapels, were not so threatened, but the Act nevertheless brought overall relief and a renewal of Unitarian confidence, and paved the way for a further period of enthusiasm and expansion.

Recovery

An immediate practical result of the Dissenters' Chapels Act was the attention given to the repair and rebuilding of meeting houses long neglected while the threat of sequestration hung over them. Trustees who had been reluctant to spend money now embarked on schemes for renovation. In other places where enthusiasm was coupled with the commercial success and advancing social status of local Unitarian magnates, new chapels were erected on a grand scale. At Hyde Chapel, Gee Cross, Cheshire, the new Gothic church, completed in 1848, was viewed as a memorial to the Dissenters' Chapels Act. A plaque over the north door records the protection it afforded to Non-subscribing dissenters. Later the same year, Mill Hill Chapel, Leeds, was also completed in the fashionable new Gothic style, which now reflected the general concern of the period with the Romantic Movement in art and literature, as well as religion. The style was in marked contrast to the Classicism of the previous century and prevailed for Unitarian rebuilding until it reached a climax with the opening of Ullet Road Church, Liverpool in 1899.

Outward confidence was, however, matched with cautious theological reserve. The bitter experience of the Wolverhampton and Lady Hewley cases now determined the way in which Unitarianism was presented. Increasingly the emphasis was placed on its non-sectarian aspects. Free religion was stressed, while Unitarian doctrinal statements tended to be discouraged. The Hibbert Trust, established in 1849, to promote Christianity in "its simplest and most intelligible form" illustrates the tendency; its deed reads as if it were non-sectarian, though there is little doubt that its promoters intended it primarily, if not exclusively, to subsidize Unitarian projects.

Similarly, when Manchester New College moved from Manchester to London in 1853, its tutors J. J. Tayler and James Martineau advanced the view that while it was correct for a Unitarian to maintain he or she was one, it was wrong to apply the term to churches or organizations. For, they argued, the basis of association in a church is not doctrinal, but one of Christian fellowship. The Unitarian name was therefore eschewed in favor of what they believed to be the catholicity of spirit represented by their English Presbyterian forebears

Conflicting Wings

Not everyone shared these views, and there were those who continued to promote Unitarianism more forthrightly. John Relly Beard and William Gaskell had in mind the provision of a different kind of ministry which would be missionary minded and popular in spirit. Its aim was to spread Unitarianism to an intelligent working-class constituency attracted to domestic missions, located in the poorer districts of the expanding industrial cities. In 1854, after Manchester New College had departed for London, they founded the Unitarian Home Missionary Board in Manchester, which became the Unitarian Home Missionary College in 1889 and the Unitarian College, Manchester, in 1926. This approach was more strident in promoting Unitarian doctrine, although it was never dogmatic.

The two approaches, one primarily serving the historic movement that derived from the liberal English Presbyterians and the other more aggressively promoting Unitarian views to a wider social constituency, tended to develop as two wings of Unitarianism. Indeed, a joke Unitarians like to tell against themselves is about a movement that has two wings, but never quite manages to fly off the ground. More seriously, the two wings characteristically provided variety of expression. There were not only two colleges, but also two hymnbooks and two denominational newspapers.

One of these, *The Inquirer*, dating from 1842, is the second oldest denominational organ in Great Britain, after the Roman Catholic *Tablet*. It was influential in promoting denominational identity, but when it sided with the theological developments led by Martineau, it led to the commencement of other journals, *The Unitarian Herald* and *The Christian Life*, to cater for the popular wing of Unitarianism.

The Christian Life was founded by Robert Spears, a former Primitive Methodist with a gift for deploying journalism in support of Unitarian extension. He was appointed secretary of the British and Foreign Unitarian Association in 1869, but resigned in 1876 when the Association decided to republish the works of Theodore Parker. Applying his testimonial fund to

Robert Spears

his new journal, for more than fifty years Spears provided a lively alternative to *The Inquirer*, promoting to the end a conservative Biblical Unitarianism, which virtually died with him 1899.

While the Dissenters' Chapels Act had secured the chapel proper-ties, it had no bearing on the Lady Hewley Case, which left the Unitarian ministry deprived of the grants it had previously received in augmentation of stipends. In 1853, of 154 ministers, eighty had stipends below £100 per annum, averaging only £54, while for the remaining seventy-four the average did not reach £150. It was to make good these losses and to remedy the impoverishment of ministers that a group of wealthy Unitarians, mainly from the Liverpool district, established the Ministers' Stipend Augmenta-tion Fund in 1856. Limited at first to ministers in England with churches north of the River Trent in the hope that other areas would make similar provision, its beneficial area was later extended.

The progress of Nonconformist emancipation that had begun with the repeal of the Test and Corporation Acts in 1828 was almost completed when religious tests for admission to Oxford, Cambridge, and Durham universities were abandoned in 1871. Only the right to be buried in a parish churchyard without Anglican rites now remained, and this was achieved in 1880. It has been suggested that this was when the synthesis which had sustained the political cohesion of Nonconformity over a period of fifty years, in the campaign for the removal of the disabilities, began to break up. It rallied again, briefly, to provide the Liberal landslide election victory in 1906, but the onset of World War I brought difficulties from which it never really recovered.

The Social Context of Nineteenth-Century Unitarian Advance

Conflicts between the rival wings of Unitarianism, and the theological changes to be described in the next chapter, took place in the context of a nation coming to terms with industrialization and urban development. Towns and cities were expanding on an unprecedented scale. London's population doubled in the first half of the century, while Manchester's more than trebled, from 75,281 in 1801 to 303,382 in 1851. Overcrowding in unsanitary dwellings resulted in high infant mortality and typhoid epidemics; while unrestrained capitalism caused the exploitation of labor, wage cutting and unemployment.

In the textile manufacturing districts of the northwest, which were heartlands of Unitarian advance, the problems were exacerbated when, in 1861, the American Civil War led to the Cotton Famine, as imports of the raw materials came to a halt.

To this instability was added the fear on the part of the middle classes, to which, in the main, Unitarians belonged, that the revolutions which occurred in many European cities throughout 1848 might be repeated in Britain if something were not done to remedy the grievances.

The novels of Elizabeth Gaskell, the wife of the minister of Cross Street Chapel, Manchester, which stressed the need for social reconciliation, for better understanding between employers and workers, between the respectable and the outcasts of society, did much to draw attention to the difficulties; as also, later in the century, did a pioneering "Survey of Life and Labour in London" (1889-1897), by another Unitarian, Charles Booth.

Unitarians were not unique in their responses, but they were proportionally well represented (usually as individuals) in a broad range of political and social reforms, including education, factory legislation, public health and reformatory schools. If they were vigorously engaged denominationally, they nonetheless found time and energy to bear witness socially.

16

Theological Developments

A radical shift in the theological basis of Unitarianism accompanied nineteenth-century organizational developments. During the first three decades, a Bible-based theology, albeit informed by the emergence of Biblical Criticism, was epitomized by the statement, in 1823, of Charles Wellbeloved, minister of St Saviourgate Chapel and Principal of Manchester College, York: "Convince us that any tenet is authorized by the Bible, from that moment we receive it ... and no power on earth shall wrest it from us."

Yet by the end of the century, reason and conscience had become the principal criteria of religious authority, with even scripture being put to this test. The changes, which did not go uncontested by a significant number of Unitarians wedded to the older traditions, stemmed mainly from the religious philosophy of James Martineau, by common consent the greatest single influence on the development of modern British Unitarianism, though now remembered more by name than for his thought.

It should be noted however that the extent to which Martineau was responsible for the turning point in nineteenth-century British Unitarianism has recently been challenged by R. K. Webb, who argues that it owed more to the anti-supernaturalism that occurred in the last third of the century, than to the earlier conflict between the Old and New Schools, represented on the one hand by Priestley and on the other by Martineau.

James Martineau

James Martineau was born at Norwich in 1805, the seventh child of a family of Huguenot origin and the younger brother of the writer and journalist Harriet Martineau. The family attended the Octagon Chapel during the ministry of Thomas Madge. After a few years at Norwich Grammar School, James went to a school at Bristol run by Lant Carpenter, the minister at Lewin's Mead Chapel. He began an engineering apprenticeship at Derby in 1821, where he lodged with the Rev. Edward Higginson, whose daughter he later married.

In 1822 Martineau decided to enter the ministry and went to Manchester College, York, a decision said to have been linked to the death of an uncle. On completion of the course he settled in Dublin as assistant minister, before moving to Paradise Street, Liverpool, where a new church was built for him at Hope Street in 1849. In 1840 he became professor at Manchester New College, which had returned to Manchester from York, where it remained until moving to London in 1853. The duties involved making the six-hour journey to Manchester for two days' teaching each fortnight. After the college moved to London he retained the Liverpool ministry until 1859, when he became minister at Little Portland Street Chapel, London, eventually succeeding J. J. Tayler as principal of the College in 1869.

The essence of Martineau's theological development was his transition from the necessarianism, determinism and materialism of Priestley and Belsham to a belief in the freedom of the spirit, and a parallel shift from rigid scriptural Unitarianism to free faith based on the inner authority of the enlightened conscience. Initially he had shared the determinist position, but the change was already evident in his *Rationale of Religious Enquiry* (1836). His subsequent life was the working out of the basic idea of the *Rationale* with reference to William Ellery Channing, Theodore Parker, and the Tübingen School of New Testament criticism.

To some extent Martineau's theology reflected the Romanticism of mid-Victorian culture, which gave greater place to intuition and feeling, compared with the earlier more cerebral approach to matters of faith. Practically, it resulted in a different form of church architecture, which might be called modified Anglican, with the once central pulpit being replaced by pulpit and reading desk, as if emphasizing the balance between the preaching and devotional elements of worship. Sermons increasingly appealed more to the emotions than specifically to the mind.

It was only in retirement, at over eighty years of age, that Martineau, spending the summers at Aviemore, in the Scottish Highlands, and the winters in London, found time to publish his mature thought in three main works. *Types of Ethical Theory* (1885) and his *Study of Religion* (1888) are

James Martineau, 1847

of lesser importance, while *The Seat of Authority in Religion* (1890) sets out in detail the position ultimately adopted by Unitarianism. It rejects all external authority, whether of Church or scripture. The subjectivism can be criticized, but Unitarians were increasingly prepared to follow him in thinking that this position represents the only really valid location of religious authority, namely in the enlightened conscience. The work also contained much New Testament criticism, including repudiation of the idea that Jesus was the Messiah. This, however, was balanced by a high regard for Jesus as "the Prince of Saints," and a conviction that personal devotion to Jesus was possible.

Among more conservative Unitarians this position did not go unchallenged. Samuel Bache, minister at the New Meeting, Birmingham and Martineau's own brother-in-law, led the opposition, even to the point of his congregation renaming their place of worship the "Church of the Messiah" when it was rebuilt in the gothic style in 1862. The title was retained until it reverted to its original name of New Meeting on a further rebuilding at Five Ways in 1973.

The new thought only served to drive further the wedge between the two wings of Unitarianism, though division was never clear cut and many convictions were held in common. In 1857, when it became necessary to reduce the staffing at Manchester New College to just two professorships, opponents initially resisted Martineau's reappointment on the grounds that he and the other chair holder, Principal J. J. Tayler, would be of the same school of thought. Moreover, though Martineau may have been theologically progressive, he was politically and socially conservative by comparison with colleagues who sought to progress Unitarianism among the new urban working class.

Martineau's profound influence on the devotional life of the movement has nonetheless been widely acknowledged, though in practice his legacy is barely discernible today. His collections of hymns *For Christian Church and Home*, 1849, and *Praise and Prayer*, 1876, have long since disappeared. His prayers, especially "Eternal God, who commitest to us the swift and solemn trust of life..." are heard occasionally, but generally are a victim of the abandonment of service book worship for more open styles. Service Seven in *Orders of Worship*, 1932, was Martineau material, but the language is Victorian, as used in worship prior to the publication of the *New English Bible* New Testament in 1961, which opened the floodgates for the use of more contemporary language.

The emphatic distinction he made between the uses of the term Unitarian as a basis for individual theology, and, in his opinion, its utter inappropriateness as a title for a church, led to his non-sectarian view of church life. Yet his Free Christian Union, 1868, failed to attract any but Unitarians and an Anglican or two, and was dissolved in 1870. A plan for the return of the Unitarian movement to a Presbyterian system of government, more imagined than real, which he presented to the triennial National Conference at Leeds in 1888, was received with a standing ovation and quickly forgotten.

Martineau may have over-emphasized the catholicity of the English Presbyterians. His fear that the Unitarian name would bind the movement to a narrow sectarianism has hardly proved to be the case. Indeed, though the Unitarian label is often misinterpreted by the orthodox as simply the holding of a sectarian Christology, for most Unitarians today, even those strongly committed to Liberal Christianity, it has become synonymous with the broad and catholic principles for which Martineau argued. He died in London in January 1900, aged 94 years.

International and Interfaith Developments

James Martineau could never understand the interest which James Estlin Carpenter, one of his successors as principal of Manchester New College, took in the study of the world religions. Before Martineau died it had become an area of increasing concern to British and American Unitarians, who played a significant part in the organization of the World Parliament of Religious held at Chicago in 1893. An outgrowth from it was the formation in Boston, Massachusetts, in 1900, of the International Council of Unitarian and Other Liberal Religious Thinkers and Workers, which became the International Association for Liberal Christianity and Religious Freedom and eventually the International Association for Religious Freedom (IARF). Until the 1950s, its membership was drawn mainly from groups with liberal Christian traditions, but afterwards it increasingly attracted member groups from Asia, the largest of which were the Japanese lay Buddhist movement Rissho Kosei-kai, and the Won Buddhists of Korea.

While the IARF has continued to promote freedom from State interference or discrimination in religion and belief, and tolerance and harmony between religious communities, it was perhaps this broader constituency that led some within the international Unitarian and Universalist communities to feel an organization was required that would more specifically foster the world-wide growth of the Unitarian and Universalist cause. The result was the formation of the International Council of Unitarians and Universalists on 25 March 1995, which now has member organizations in more than twenty countries worldwide.

17

Toward a New Century

The Unitarian movement was too deeply rooted in liberal traditions for Martineau's new theological departure to result in secession, even though his theological stance was vigorously challenged. On the contrary, the vibrancy of the debate, coupled with increased financial support from successful Unitarian manufacturing, shipping and business dynasties, resulted in a period of growth extending from the mid-nineteenth century until at least the 1870s. District missionary associations, which have become today's District Associations, were formed to promote new congregations and revive old ones, and increasingly, if slowly, financial support for the whole movement came from local sources.

The restoration of old chapels, which had been neglected during the protracted Lady Hewley litigation, continued apace. Between 1839 and 1900, 111 places of worship were built or rebuilt. Seventy-two of them were completed after 1870, which suggests that decline came later. Most of them were free from mortgage even though the ending of the mid-Victorian economic boom in 1873 must have reduced the incomes of subscribers. Moreover, the installation of gas lighting led to the introduction of evening services and popular styles of worship, which aimed to attract working people who were unlikely to feel comfortable with the wealthy, carriage-riding pillars of society who attended in the mornings. Even where old meetinghouses were retained, new ancillary brick buildings arose to accommodate Sunday Schools and a growing range of educational and social activities.

Denominational Identity

Denominational identity was promoted by the introduction of a British and Foreign Unitarian Association Sunday, held annually from 1883

110

onwards. To encourage expansion in Scotland, William McQuaker made a substantial bequest to the British and Foreign Unitarian Association in 1889 to diffuse the principles of Unitarian Christianity north of the border and to supplement ministers' salaries in non-self-supporting congregations. Popular lectures were also arranged in cities and large towns. The Essex Hall Lecture, hardly regarded as "popular" discourse today, survives as a feature of present-day General Assembly Meetings. National identity also acquired its focus in the adaptation of Lindsey's Essex Street Chapel to provide offices for the British and Foreign Unitarian Association and the Sunday School Association, though it would be a long time before anyone would call it a headquarters.

The early twentieth century was also a period of staunch Unitarian commitment to social reform. A Union of Social Service was established in 1904, similar to those in the other Free Church denominations. The triennial National Conference of 1891 was devoted to "The Church and Social Questions," no doubt in response to the emergence of an Independent Labour movement at that time. In keeping with liberal social concerns of the day, a Unitarian Temperance Association was established in 1893 to consolidate the work of the various bands of hope existing in connection with the churches. It was presided over by a rarity in Unitarian circles, a peer of the realm, albeit a rather eccentric one – the Earl of Carlisle, who from his seat at Castle Howard attended the Unitarian Chapel at Malton, Yorkshire.

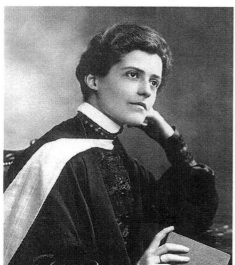

Gertrud von Petzold
In 1904 she became the first woman
to have full ministerial status in any
British denomination

In 1904, the movement took the pioneering step of admitting the Rev. Gertrud von Petzold into its ministry at Narborough Road Free Christian (Unitarian) Church, Leicester, the first woman to be so acknowledged on the roll of any British religious denomination.

Pioneer Preachers, Free Catholic Movement and the Van Mission

A desire to bridge the social divide led to the adoption of popular propagandist techniques similar to those being used by the political parties. The Unitarian Van Mission, the brainchild of T. P. Spedding, from 1905 deployed horse-drawn caravans, crewed by volunteer missioners, to tour the country spreading the Unitarian message in areas where there were few Unitarian chapels. More eccentric was the witness of the Rev. Douglas Muir, who in 1920 took to the road as Friar Douglas, the first and possibly the last Unitarian friar. Starting his wanderings in sandals and habit, he quickly returned to more conventional dress. He had perhaps not counted the cost, as soon nothing more was heard of this colorful and dramatic experiment. Other popular propagandist initiatives included the Central Postal Mission, organized almost entirely by women, and the deployment of demountable iron churches, which in theory could be taken apart and moved to a new location when a congregation was well established.

Two other early twentieth-century movements were linked with the general intention to widen the social constituency of Unitarianism in the years before World War I. The Order of the Brotherhood of the Pioneer Preachers grew out of R. J. Campbell's New Theology movement, which popularized a Modernist Christianity derived from the progress of late nineteenth-century liberal Biblical criticism. When Campbell recanted and returned to the folds of orthodoxy, the Pioneer Preachers, who had found their most receptive audiences among Unitarians, became more closely associated with the movement. Many of them entered the ministry through the Unitarian Home Missionary College at Manchester. They became prominent leaders throughout the twentieth century, their left-wing politics and popular ministries having particular appeal to northern congregations.

The Free Catholic Movement had a corporate life between 1916 and 1928, and was most visible in its small magazine *The Free Catholic*. Generally, it attracted a different kind of minister than the Pioneer Preachers. The leading exponent was J. M. Lloyd Thomas, minister of the Old Meeting, Birmingham. Its adherents emphasized the "catholic" basis of the English Presbyterians, particularly Richard Baxter. They were not all attached to Unitarianism, and those who were tended to eschew the term and regarded themselves and their congregations as "Free Christian." The group included J. S. Burgess (Flowery Field), Stanley Mellor (Hope Street,

Unitarian Van Mission
ready for a meeting

Liverpool), F. Heming Vaughan (Gee Cross), W. Whitaker (Platt) and
H. H. Johnson (Evesham). It has been argued that only J. Lloyd Thomas
applied his Free Catholic principles to a local congregation, but it is impossible to evaluate congregations like Gee Cross and Flowery Field, Hyde,
where a crucifix still hangs over the pulpit and there is a reluctance to use
the Unitarian name, without reference to Free Catholic influence.

The National Conference, 1882 and the General Assembly, 1928

The establishment of Unitarian denominational identity, over the looser and unorganized association of congregations that was characteristic of the movement up to the end of the eighteenth century, was completed in two stages: first by the formation of the National Conference of Unitarian, Liberal Christian, Free Christian, Presbyterian and other Non-Subscribing Congregations, in 1882, then by the establishment of the General Assembly of Unitarian and Free Christian Churches in 1928.

The National Conference resulted partly from the failure of James Martineau's short-lived Free Christian Union. It was a triennial gathering for fellowship and discussion, meeting first in Liverpool and finally at Sheffield in 1926. No authority was vested in it and it had no financial base. Its officers were all honorary, and expenses of the meetings were borne by the host churches. Membership consisted of the minister and one delegate from each church on the roll. Founded by the British and Foreign Unitarian Association, because the Association itself was regarded as too propagandist and sectarian, the intention was a broader association than had previously been achieved. These hopes were not fulfilled, however, and the constituency of the National Conference remained exactly the same as the churches listed in the British and Foreign Unitarian Association's *Essex Hall Year Book*.

The formation of the General Assembly in 1928 resulted mainly from increasing tension between the National Conference and the British and Foreign Unitarian Association. This had almost produced a split at the Conference held at Bolton in 1909, but reconciling tendencies after World War I led to a movement for amalgamation. Moreover there was a winding down of the clash between the "old" Unitarians and the Martineau supporters. Annual meetings were first held at Manchester in 1929. A good popular account of them, up to 1945, is given in R. P. Jones's *It is Very Observable*. With the sole exception of Old Meeting, Birmingham, where J. M. Lloyd Thomas, a leading member of the Free Catholic Movement, was minister, all existing congregations became members, including those of the Non-Subscribing Presbyterian Church of Ireland, which had been formed in 1910. Of the ministers, only Lloyd Thomas and L. P. Jacks, the principal of Manchester College, Oxford, actively opposed the scheme, but one or two others, including Alexander Gordon, by then retired, also withheld their names from the new assembly's Roll of Ministers.

After the formation of the General Assembly, the British and Foreign Unitarian Association (an incorporated body since 1915) continued to be the official legal arm of the Assembly and today acts as Custodian Trustee for several Unitarian congregations and trusts, though some of this work is now done by District Associations, who have registered themselves as incorporated bodies.

Unity within the Assembly also led to cooperation in a number of specific areas. The new status which women were assuming in society, and the social developments heralded by the Liberal landslide victory in the 1906 General Election, coupled with agitations for the female franchise, were no doubt factors in the formation of the Women's League in 1908. The Unitarian Men's League provided similar fellowship for the men. For younger people the Fellowship of Youth (FOY Society), founded in 1923, provided a national association, though it tended to cater mainly for the offspring of well-to-do Unitarians, who went up to university, eschewing anything too closely associated with overt Unitarianism. Less privileged young people, whose circumstances generally limited them to employment in their home-towns, had to await the formation of the Unitarian Young Peoples' League in 1934 for their sense of corporate identity. When it came, it was a vibrant movement, which would be a seedbed of Unitarian leaders to serve the movement in lay and ministerial positions up to the present day.

Unitarianism in the twentieth century has shared the numerical decline associated with the general marginalization of organized religion in Great Britain. After the disruptions of World War II, including the bombing and subsequent rebuilding of Essex Hall, the postwar period saw the launching of two major appeals for £100,000 and £200,000 in support of the Assembly, and also the foundation of the National Unitarian Fellowship to cater for isolated Unitarians.

The only significant development in structures at this time was the promotion of Fellowships, whereby new Unitarian congregations were founded, providing worship and fellowship without the heavy and increasingly expensive responsibilities of maintaining church buildings. The idea was borrowed from similar developments in the United States. Few were more than short-lived, though they were vibrant for a time. Watford Unitarian Fellowship (1947) in Watford, Hertfordshire, has survived, providing a model for similar groups at a later date, and for newly emergent groups today. Whether or not the original intention was for Fellowships to become Churches with their own premises, none did so.

To the spectrum of theological stances, which before the war might have been summed up as broadly Liberal Christian or Theistic, was now added a more vocal humanism. Although the latter has perhaps been exaggerated because of developments in the United States, it nonetheless produced a reaction in the formation of the Fellowship of Liberal Christians. There was also a trend toward worship that incorporated the sacred writings of the world faiths, inspired by Will Hayes of Chatham, whose service book was *Every Nation Kneeling*. Behind this tendency lay Estlin Carpenter's pioneering interests in world religions, and ahead of it was a Britain becoming increasingly multicultural and multi-religious.

In the General Assembly, the attempt to acknowledge the Judeo-Christian heritage, while at the same time coming to terms with this pluralist ethos, found expression in debates about the object of the organization. After several years of deliberation, in April 2001 the Assembly adopted the following statement:

> We, the constituent congregations, affiliated societies and individual members, uniting in a spirit of mutual sympathy, co-operation, tolerance and respect; and recognising the worth and dignity of all people and their freedom to believe as their consciences dictate; and believing that truth is best served where the mind and conscience are free, acknowledge that the Object of the Assembly is:
>
> To promote a free and inquiring religion through the worship of God and the celebration of life; the service of humanity and respect for all creation; and the upholding of the liberal Christian tradition.
>
> To this end, the Assembly may: Encourage and unite in fellowship bodies which uphold the religious liberty of their members, unconstrained by the imposition of creeds;
>
> Affirm the liberal religious heritage and learn from the spiritual, cultural and intellectual insights of all humanity;
>
> Act where necessary as the successor to the British and Foreign Unitarian Association and National Conference of Unitarian, Liberal Christian, Free Christian, Presbyterian and other Non-Subscribing or Kindred Congregations, being faithful to the spirit of their work and principles (see appendix to the constitution), providing always that this shall in no way limit the complete doctrinal freedom of the constituent churches and members of the Assembly;
>
> Do all other such lawful things as are incidental to the attainment of the above Object.

Essex Hall, on the site of Lindsey's Essex Street Chapel
Headquarters of the General Assembly of Unitarian and Free Christian Churches

PART 3

AMERICA

18

Origins

The emergence of a Unitarian movement in America was not simply a colonial outgrowth from the movement in Britain, any more than British Unitarianism is explained only by influences from continental Europe. Claims for independent beginnings in Britain and America are a little too neat, even if broadly correct. It is true, however, that Unitarianism arose in different countries and continents not simply because the word of it spread with travel and communications, but because social and religious conditions made it timely for a particular place.

Colonial connections there were, but American Unitarianism was largely a product of American conditions. Earl Morse Wilbur points out that Socinian thought and literature had little influence in America, and that the movement there was of indigenous origin, largely independent in its earliest stages of similar tendencies in England. Conrad Wright echoes this view by suggesting the roots lay deep in New England Puritanism, yet acknowledges that English Latitudinarianism and dissent helped to shape the growth of Unitarianism in the United States.

The Unitarian movements on either side of the Atlantic developed out of different traditions of church polity. In Great Britain, Unitarianism was primarily a doctrinal development from the Arminianism of the English Presbyterians. To this were added Lindsey's resignation from the Church of England and the late-eighteenth and nineteenth-century accessions of the General Baptists, the Methodist Unitarians, and the Christian Brethren. In America, Unitarianism grew mainly from the Congregational churches of New England, to which were added congregations founded by British immigrants in the mid-Atlantic and southern states.

New England Congregationalism: Separatism and Puritanism

New England Congregationalism was a fusion of Separatism and Puritanism. The Pilgrims who settled at Plymouth, Massachusetts, in 1620 represented Separatism. They had separated from the Church of England on principle because Separatism was the New Testament model of the church, and they had emigrated because of the persecution this brought upon them. Sailing from England in the *Mayflower*, they went first to Holland, thence to America, where they created an establishment of Separatist congregations. The church they founded at Plymouth has subsequently become Unitarian, the fifth building on the original site.

Puritanism was represented by the colonies at Salem and Massachusetts Bay. Although not Separatist, they were equally committed to a Congregational form of church government.

First Sunday in New England, after a painting by Alfed Walter Bayes

The Cambridge Platform of 1648 defined the constitution and polity of these New England churches. It was a declaration of Independency in opposition to Presbyterianism. Each autonomous church, under the guidance of the Holy Spirit, called its own minister. Conrad Wright has identified it as "a bold attempt to make the civil and political society identical with the spiritual or religious society."

Although Congregational rather that Presbyterian, the churches were strictly Calvinist in their doctrine, holding that some people, the elect, were predestined to eternal life and others, the damned, to eternal death, by God's decree. While there was no precise way of knowing who was in each category, they acted as if they could distinguish. Only the elect could be church members, and only church members could be the freemen who took part in the government of the Colony. This situation prevailed as late as 1674 when there were only 2,537 men, all of them church members, who could exercise the franchise in the state of Massachusetts.

Liberal Religious Thought Penetrates a Calvinist Society

The question now arises, how did liberal religious ideas, ultimately leading to Unitarianism, penetrate this rigidly Calvinist society? It is a conundrum which echoes the incredible reversal that took place in Great Britain during the eighteenth century, whereby the once Calvinist Presbyterians became liberal non-subscribers, while the once free Antinomian Independents became orthodox.

One answer is found in the Congregational system, which had no overriding authority to easily stamp out heresy. Another is provided by the non-dogmatic covenants on which the churches were based. These derived from the original covenant that the Pilgrim Fathers adopted for themselves on their arrival at Plymouth, as the basis of their association. This was recorded by William Bradford in his *History of Plymouth Plantation*:

> The Lord's free people joyned themselves into a church state, in the fellowship of the gospell, to walk in all [God's] ways made known or to be made known unto them, according to their best endeavour, whatever it should cost them.

This was revised in 1676, without any radical change in character or substance, and has remained the basis of the religious society of the First Parish Church, Plymouth, now Unitarian:

> We do here solemnly and religiously, as in his most holy presence, avouch the Lord Jehovah, the only true God, to be our God and the God of ours; and do promise and bind ourselves to walk in all our ways according to the rule of the gospel, and in all sincere conformity to his holy ordinances, and in mutual love and watchfulness over one another, depending wholly upon the Lord our God to enable us by his grace hereunto.

Another example of a non-dogmatic covenant is the one made for the church at Salem in 1629. Although the congregation altered it in 1636 to define ways of practical piety, they made no doctrinal additions.

> We covenant with the Lord and with one another, and doe bind ourselves in the presence of God, to walk together in all his waies, according as he is pleased to reveal himself unto us in his blessed word of truth.

Similarly, the covenant of 1630 for First Church, Boston, was and remains:

> [We] do hereby solemnly and religiously promise and bind ourselves to walk in all our ways according to the rule of the gospel, and in all sincere conformity to [Christ's] holy ordinances, and in mutual love and respect each to other, so near as God shall give us grace.

All of these early New England Congregational covenants agree that the supreme authority is the spirit of God. There is no form of creed. Subscribing to a covenant not only made men (and the subscribers were all males) members of the church, but also citizens of their parish. Although the covenants are remarkably modern in tone and present few difficulties for religious liberals today, one must be careful not to read into them a liberal outlook that was not intended. For they were not deliberately framed to allow new doctrinal interpretation, any more than were the open trust deeds of the English meetinghouses. Doctrinal orthodoxy was presumed. However, because the covenants contained nothing to forbid doctrinal development, they left open the way for subsequent changes. No one could appeal to them in order to denounce a new teaching. Thus, when churches founded by the Pilgrim Fathers and the Puritan colonists became more liberal, and ultimately Unitarian, there was no need to replace the covenants. Indeed, today each of the these churches continues under its original covenant.

For decades after their foundation the Congregational churches of New England held firmly and resolutely to orthodox Calvinist theology. Laws passed against heresy, however, were directed mainly at other denominations: Roman Catholics, Episcopalians, Quakers, and Baptists.

Had these churches succeeded in establishing their ideal, a complete unity of the temporal and spiritual, they might have created in New England one of the most rigid and authoritarian institutions in history. This did not occur for two reasons.

First, voices were raised against Puritan intolerance. Sir Richard Saltonstall, a settler who returned to England to escape persecution, wrote:

> It does not a little grieve my spirit to hear what sad things are reported of your tyranny and persecution in New England as that you fine, whip and imprison men for their consciences – truly, this your practice of compelling any [in] matters of worship to do that whereof they are not persuaded is to make them sin and many are hypocrites thereby conforming in their outward man for fear of punishment.

In 1650 William Pynchon denied that Christ was subject to the wrath of God, or that he suffered torments in hell for human redemption. Pynchon's book, *The Meritorious Price of our Redemption*, was condemned to be burnt by the common hangman in the marketplace in Boston. Like Saltonstall, he returned to England, driven out by the prevailing atmosphere. Roger Williams, minister at Salem, was banished from Massachusetts for his robust defense of spiritual freedom. He maintained that civil power had no jurisdiction over conscience. His principles became the basis of the Rhode Island colony, which, in advance of other colonies, held that all individuals and all religious societies – pagans, Christians, or Jews – were entitled to religious liberty. Thus, in 1651, Rhode Island refused to join with the United Colonies in the persecution of Quakers.

Second, a state church on the Puritan pattern was prohibited by the nature of New England Congregationalism. Attempts to secure uniformity of belief and practice ran contrary to the spirit of Independency, which rested upon revelation given to individual believers. In principle every church member had the right to interpret spiritual truth for himself. He was admitted to church membership on the basis of his own testimony of personal conversion. When, at Boston in 1680, a synod representing five colonies adopted a confession of faith based on the Savoy Confession of 1658, an abridgement of the Westminster Confession, the principle of Independency prevented its imposition on the individual churches. Congregational autonomy meant that each church must be left free to adopt it or not. Some did not.

In these circumstances a liberal movement emerged, which was referred to as Arminian, taking its name from the Dutch theologian Jacob Arminius, who believed, contrary to the predestinarian orthodox Calvinists, that all individuals had the free will to accept or reject God's grace.

19

The Arminian Movement

The gradual development of a liberal "Arminian" movement, which began as a response to the rigid Calvinism of the New England churches, was influenced by seventeenth and eighteenth-century English latitudinarian thought. New England divines read John Milton, William Chillingworth, and John Tillotson in the seventeenth century. In the eighteenth century they read William Whiston, Samuel Clarke, and Thomas Emlyn.

The Great Awakening of 1734

Prior to the Great Awakening – a wave of Evangelical fervor that swept through New England in 1734-35, corresponding to the Evangelical Revival in Great Britain and to Pietism in Europe – orthodox theology had gone virtually unchallenged. Cotton Mather, a leader of the Puritan clergy, said of the New England churches in 1726 that "they perfectly adhere to the Confession of Faith published by the Assembly of Divines at Westminster and afterward renewed by the Synod of Savoy ... I cannot learn that among all the pastors of two hundred churches there is one Arminian, much less an Arian, or a Gentilist." Whether or not that was truly the case, the Awakening crystallized doctrinal opinion into orthodox and liberal wings.

The Great Awakening began spontaneously at the end of 1734. Jonathan Edwards, the minister at Northampton, Massachusetts, guided its spiritual fervor and gave it an intellectual base. George Whitefield, the English revivalist, who had previously assisted John Wesley during his years in America, raised it to even higher levels of emotional enthusiasm.

Underlying the Awakening, and its religious confrontation, was economic and social cleavage. The revivalist supporters tended to be of a lower social class, while those who resisted it most vigorously were the intellectual and mercantile elite of Boston and other seaboard towns. The focus of resistance was Harvard College, which upheld an unemotional, reasonable, and tolerant approach to religion. Yet Harvard was not alone in opposition. There were two other important spheres of Arminian influence: in Connecticut, centering on Yale College, and Rhode Island, a Baptist stronghold, where ministers generally had no college training, but strongly upheld traditions of religious liberty.

The Reaction: Arminian, Rational, and Liberal

The liberals who resisted revivalism and the Evangelical theology of the Great Awakening increasingly found common ground as Arminians. Gradually casting off Calvinist orthodoxy, they displayed three main theological tendencies.

Their doctrine of human nature was Arminian. Arminians asserted that people are born with a capacity both for sin and righteousness. Individuals can respond to the impulse to holiness as well as to temptation. Life is a process of trial and discipline through which bondage to sin can be overcome. Compared to orthodox Calvinist belief in total human depravity and in predestination to either damnation or eternal happiness, it was an optimistic outlook. It offered the possibility of salvation to all who would accept the free grace of God in Jesus Christ.

The Arminians were also Rationalists. They asserted that unassisted reason could establish the essentials of natural religion, the existence of God, and the obligations of morality. Natural religion must, nonetheless, be supplemented by the special revelation of God's will given in the Bible. They opposed creeds and confessions of faith as being of human origin. Moreover, Arminians tended to be anti-Trinitarian in Christology. Most were Arians, believing that Jesus was not God, but a divine being higher in creation than man.

The leaders of the movement influenced subsequent generations of ministers. Ebenezer Gay, sometimes called the "Father of American Unitarianism," was for sixty-nine years minister at Hingham, Massachusetts. Long ministries suggest positions of strong independency. Ministers' stipends were supported by the taxation of all property in the parish. Incumbents could only be removed for serious offences. That Gay and several other liberal ministers served for more than fifty years, baptizing, marrying, and burying two or three generations of parishioners, helps to explain the transition of whole congregations from Calvinism to Unitarianism. In a letter of 15 May 1815, John Adams, the second President of the United States and member of the First Church at Quincy, described Gay as a Unitarian.

Jonathan Mayhew, pastor of the West Church in Boston from 1747 until his death, preached against the revival and declared that the Bible alone was the test of the new teaching. He was the first of the New England clergy to publicly oppose the doctrine of the Trinity. Insisting on the unity of God, he declared that it was a just reproach to Christians that they had ceased to give sole worship to the Father. His Christology was more Arian than Socinian. He preferred to leave Christ's nature undefined, as it was

Jonathan Mayhew, minister of West Church, Boston
The first of the New England clergy to oppose the doctrine of the Trinity

in the New Testament. He maintained that Christianity was not a scheme of salvation defined by dogma, but the art of living virtuously and piously. As most Boston ministers refused to participate in his ordination, he had to appeal to those in nearby country parishes.

Charles Chauncy, for sixty years the minister of Boston's First Church, led the opposition to Whitefield's revivalist methods. Having a somewhat prosaic mind, he is said to have expressed the wish that someone should translate Milton's *Paradise Lost* into prose so that he might understand it. He despised rhetoric and prayed never to become an orator. This prayer, a friend teasingly said, seemed to have been answered. His publications included *Enthusiasm Described and Cautioned Against* (1742) and *Seasonable Thoughts on the State of Religion in New England* (1743).

Charles Chauncy, minister of First Church, Boston
He led the opposition to George Whitefield's revivalist methods

The emergence and decline of the Great Awakening can be gauged by the relative successes and failures of George Whitefield's visits. At the end of his first campaign in 1740 he is said to have given a farewell discourse to 20,000 people on Boston Common. His second visit in 1744 was less successful, possibly as a result of the counterattack by the Arminians. In 1754 he met with little response.

King's Chapel, Boston and British Influence

Significant as was this liberal theological development within Congregationalism, it was, in fact, circumstances within an Episcopal church, which led to the first specifically Unitarian congregation in America: King's Chapel, Boston. This was another parallel with Unitarian events in England: Lindsey's pioneering Essex Street Chapel had stemmed from Anglicanism, not Dissent.

King's Chapel had been founded in 1686 for English officers wishing to worship using the *Book of Common Prayer*. It was closed in 1776 after the American Revolution led to the departure of the last Royal Governor. The building was used by the congregation of the Old South Church, before being reopened for Episcopalian worship in 1783.

At the reopening, as no Anglican clergyman could be found to serve as minister, the liberal James Freeman was installed as lay reader. He had intended to enter the Congregational ministry, but had a liking for

Anglican liturgy. The Trinitarian formulae in the liturgy soon compelled him to address the issue of the Trinity and to reject it. The majority of proprietors (trustees) supported his stance, twenty for and seven against. Thus, in June 1785, a new doctrinal basis was established for King's Chapel. The Thirty-Nine Articles, the Athanasian and Nicene Creeds, and the Trinitarian formulae were abandoned, and a version of Samuel Clarke's revised *Book of Common Prayer* introduced.

King's Chapel, Boston, circa 1910

Freeman then sought ordination. When it was obvious that this would not be forthcoming at the hands of any Anglican bishop, in November 1787 the Vestry (a lay committee) ordained him themselves. This highly controversial act was contrary to Episcopalian practice, but not irregular in the context of the dominant New England Congregationalism. Freeman was responsible for the spread of English Unitarian ideas, particularly those of Priestley. These had a strong influence at Salem, where the three churches were liberal and the ministers, William Bentley, John Prince, and Thomas Barnard, each quietly adopted Unitarian theology far earlier than did the liberal ministry in other New England towns.

A few other Unitarian congregations, established in the wake of the American Revolution and swelled by British Rational Dissenters fleeing the opposition to them in the United Kingdom at the time of the French Revolution, followed the lead of King's Chapel. In Maine the Episcopalian Thomas Oxnard founded an explicitly Unitarian congregation in Portland,

and Samuel Thatcher one at Saco. John Butler, a layman from Bristol, gave lectures in New York on the Unity of God and, in 1794, founded the short-lived First Unitarian Society of New York. Joseph Priestley's arrival in America led to the establishment of congregations at Northumberland and Philadelphia, Pennsylvania. At Northumberland, meetings were held at the home of Priestley or of his son. In 1797, at Priestley's instigation, a permanent church was organized in Philadelphia, to which, in 1806, William Christie, a Scottish disciple of Priestley's, was called as minister.

While not denying that American Unitarianism stems primarily from New England Congregationalism, two recent studies, John Macaulay's *Unitarianism in the Antebellum South: The Other Invisible Institution* and J. D. Bowers' *Joseph Priestley and English Unitarianism in America*, nonetheless argue that the conventional view requires modification in the light of the evidence they provide for the promotion of alternative versions of Unitarianism, one by Priestley and his successors in Pennsylvania, and the other in the Southern states.

Macaulay notes that quite apart from the differences between Southern and Northern Unitarians over the question of slavery, other divisions, theological, social, and political, had long stood in the way of unity. Moreover, by representation in literary, journalistic and professional spheres, Southern Unitarians had exercised an influence independent of New England, in what his subtitle calls the "Other Invisible Institution," an allusion to the hidden African American religious practices of the pre-Civil War period. Here, Macaulay maintains, the seminal influences were English Unitarianism, Jeffersonian religious liberalism, regional Arminian traditions, latitudinarianism, the quest for the primitive church, and, most importantly, "Scottish Common Sense Realism."

Bowers argues that the New England liberals deliberately suppressed the English influence of Priestley because of its strident Socinianism, which would have caused too great a breach with the mainstream churches, which the liberals wished to avoid. When William Ellery Channing declared for "Unitarian Christianity" in his sermon at Baltimore in 1819, it was for a different kind of Unitarianism, which distanced itself from the out-and-out "humanitarian" Socinian views that Priestley represented. The opposition prevailed, maintains Bowers, until the 1840s, when Theodore Parker's transcendentalist radicalism threatened the acceptability of Unitarianism as a feature of American religious life and it became preferable to acknowledge Priestley's humanitarian Christianity, rather than Parker's humanism.

It will be some time before this reassessment of the relative influence of English immigrant Unitarians on the development of Unitarianism in the United States is properly critiqued, to examine whether the claims of Macaulay and Bowers are exaggerated. Meanwhile, it may be noted that some scholars are suggesting that American Unitarian origins may not be quite so singular as they have previously been depicted.

20

The Unitarian Controversy

By ordaining James Freeman and adopting Samuel Clarke's revised *Book of Common Prayer*, King's Chapel, Boston, had effectively become a Unitarian church, if not in name. Yet, though one or two congregations followed its lead, the Congregational churches had not generally at this stage progressed further than an informal division into liberal and evangelical wings. Few, if any, congregations or ministers had gone beyond Arianism. They remained within the Standing Order of the Churches of New England.

Two events were to occur which would drive a wedge between the liberals and the evangelicals. The first was the need to make new appointments at Harvard College to fill the offices of Hollis Professor of Divinity and the Presidency of the College, and the second was the publication in America of Thomas Belsham's *Memoirs of Theophilus Lindsey*.

The Battle for Control of Harvard

In 1803, a week before the commencement of the new session at Harvard College, David Tappan died. He was a moderate Calvinist who had occupied the Hollis chair of Divinity. The question arose, who should succeed him? The election of his successor was in the hands of the Corporation of the College, six votes in all. The result required confirmation by the College's Overseers. As meeting after meeting produced no result, there was an impasse. Then, in 1804, Harvard's problem was compounded by the death of the College president, Dr. Joseph Willard. There were then two important vacancies. Would Calvinists retain these offices, or would liberals take them over?

Controversy centered on the precise terms of the gift of the Chair endowed by Thomas Hollis in 1721. This prescribed that the post should be held by "a man of solid learning in divinity, of sound and orthodox principles." On the face of it, this could not be stretched to encompass an Arminian or an anti-Trinitarian candidate – or so the evangelicals contended. The liberals, to the other hand, maintained that it did not matter whether the candidates were Calvinists, Arians, Socinians or Latitudinarians, as long as they were pious, learned, and moral men. The upshot was that two liberals were elected: the Hollis chair went to Henry Ware, the minister at Hingham, successor to Ebenezer Gay, while Samuel Webber was named as the new president.

These elections had several results. First, they ignited the Unitarian Controversy, which would ultimately result in the separation of the evangelical and liberal wings of the Congregational churches. Second, they ensured the liberal tradition at Harvard University. Third, they prompted the resignation of Jedidiah Morse as an overseer of the College. Morse, with Eliphalet Pearson, went on, in 1808, to found Andover Theological Seminary, with the express purpose of training evangelical ministers. The new seminary's teachers were required to assent to a doctrinal statement. (In 1908 Andover moved to Cambridge, Massachusetts and later merged with Newton Theological Institution, a Baptist seminary, to form Andover Newton Theological School.)

Jedidiah Morse's Challenge to the Liberals

Before the Unitarian Controversy, New England liberals had avoided the name Unitarian, though their Arianism was in fact approaching that position. They were reluctant to be identified with the thoroughgoing humanitarian Christology associated with Joseph Priestley and Thomas Belsham in England. They preferred to be called either liberals or Rational Christians. Their silence about the nature of Jesus was nevertheless frequently misconstrued. In the end, they had to acknowledge themselves Unitarian in order to distinguish themselves from their opponents.

Jedidiah Morse became the leading opponent of the liberals. His journal, the *Panoplist*, was pledged to use "the full panoply of war against the infidels." The liberals established their own rallying ground by forming the Anthology Club in 1804. It had fourteen members, six of whom were ministers. Its organ, *The Monthly Anthology*, was the first liberal and critical journal of any note in America, and the first of five liberal magazines founded in this period, including the *General Repository* and the *Christian Disciple*.

In 1812 Thomas Belsham, the minister at Essex Street Chapel, London, published his *Memoirs of Theophilus Lindsey*, to which he appended a letter from William Wells of Boston, "with some account of the present state of the Unitarians in New England." Three years later Morse republished this appendix verbatim, together with a new preface, under the title *American Unitarianism.* Having affixed the label "Unitarian" to the Boston liberals, he hoped to force them to sever their connection with the Congregational churches. In a review of *American Unitarianism*, Morse's friend Jeremiah Evarts, writing in the *Panoplist*, sought to show that the liberals were Unitarian and therefore heretics, that they conspired in secret to overthrow the true faith, and that they should be exposed and expelled from the church.

In the first liberal response, a rather cautious open letter to William C. Thatcher, minister of the New South Church in Boston, William Ellery Channing argued that, while many ministers and members of their churches were in fact Unitarian, they did not embrace Belsham's Unitarianism, which made Christ a man. While the New England liberals did not accept the Trinity, they nonetheless retained an exalted view of Jesus. And they made no open declaration of Unitarianism, not because they were operating in secret, but because they disliked the sectarian spirit and were unwilling to indulge in any form of proselytizing. The evangelicals viewed this reply suspiciously as "theological reserve" and deemed it unsatisfactory.

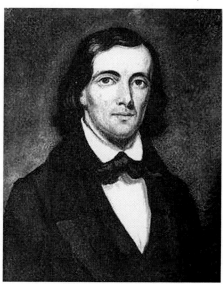

William Ellery Channing

The significance of Channing as the founding father of American Unitarianism cannot be overestimated. Revered in his day, both in America and Europe, he was born of Calvinist stock in Rhode Island in April 1780. He went to Harvard to study law at the age of 14 and returned in 1802 for divinity. His entire ministry was at Federal Street Church, Boston (now Arlington Street Church). Never of robust health, he died in 1842, aged 62 years.

Although liberal in outlook, Channing remained theologically reserved until the delivery of his Baltimore sermon in 1819, when he forthrightly declared for Unitarianism. A socially radical preacher, he was nonetheless a somewhat late convert to the antislavery campaign. It took a visit to the West Indies to arouse his concern. He eventually became a leading abolitionist.

Channing also expressed his social radicalism through the support he gave to his fellow Harvard student, Dr. Joseph Tuckerman, who, in the 1840s, headed the Ministry to the Poor. This ministry, started in 1822, was a response to the poverty of the Boston underclass, their neglect by the clergy, and their alienation from the churches. In 1826, under the direction of the American Unitarian Association, it became the Benevolent Fraternity of Churches. Although non-sectarian, it was exclusively supported by Unitarians. A visit by Tuckerman to England led to the formation of the Manchester Domestic Mission in 1833, followed by similar experiments in London, 1835; Liverpool, 1836; Bristol, 1839; and Birmingham, 1840.

Dr. Joseph Tuckerman
Pioneer of the Ministry to the Poor

Channing's Baltimore Sermon

When he preached a sermon on "Unitarian Christianity" at the ordination of Jared Sparks on May 5, 1819, Channing at last defended the Unitarian position and acknowledged the Unitarian name. The location was significant, as Baltimore was one of the largest cities south of New York, in an area where it was difficult for liberals to find a hearing. The published sermon went to eight editions in three months. According to Earl Morse Wilbur, it "had a wider, deeper, and more lasting influence than any sermon ever preached in America." This may have been so, at least until "I have a dream" was preached by Martin Luther King, Jr.

In the first part of the sermon, Channing dealt with the principles that New England Unitarians adopted in interpreting the scriptures. These, he said, are the record of God's successive revelations to humankind. The last, most perfect revelation was Jesus Christ. Unitarians are prepared to receive, without reserve or exception, whatever doctrines are taught in the scriptures, though they do not attach equal importance to all the books. The Old Testament belongs, rather, to the childhood of the human race. Jesus is the only master of Christians. What Jesus taught, or what he taught through his inspired apostles, Unitarians regarded as having divine authority. Channing's observation – that scripture must be read critically, as one would read any other book – anticipates by a half century Benjamin Jowett's memorable phrase "a book like any other book" in *Essays and Reviews*, 1869.

Part two of the sermon addressed the views that Unitarians derived from the Bible. The first of these was the unity of God, who is "one being, one mind, one person, one intelligent agent." Channing rejected the Trinity because it subverts God's unity, which is taught in scripture. The biblical phrases, "God sent his son" and "God anointed Jesus," he thought inexplicable if Jesus is God. Second was the unity of Jesus, who has "one mind, one being, one soul as all men have" and is, therefore, "distinct from God as all men are distinct from God." Third was the moral perfection of God, who "is infinitely good, kind and benevolent, good not to a few, but to every individual." This marked a definite break with the Calvinism in which Channing had been reared. Fourth, on the mediation of Christ and the purpose of his mission, Channing listed several ways through which Jesus redeems humankind. These include his teaching about God's unity, fatherhood, and moral perfection; the light he throws on the path of duty; his example; his sufferings and death; his resurrection, which was the bringing in of a future life; his intercessions; his power to raise the dead, to judge the world, and to confer everlasting rewards on the faithful.

Very different from modern Unitarianism, Channing's theology provided American Unitarians with a platform around which they could rally. It put them, for the first time, on the offensive against the orthodox. Yet it is ironic that a minister who was so anti-sectarian should have been instrumental in setting the course for a separate Unitarian denomination.

A number of subsidiary theological controversies were begun by the Baltimore Sermon, including one on the doctrine of the Trinity, between

Moses Stuart of Andover and Andrews Norton of Harvard, and one on Calvinism, between Leonard Woods of Andover and Henry Ware of Harvard. The latter was known as the Woods 'n Ware controversy.

Channing's Baltimore Sermon signaled a fresh departure for American Unitarians. It clarified the lines of division between liberals and conservatives. Yet, it would not be theology, but an 1820 legal judgment, that finally brought about the formal separation of the Unitarians from the Congregationalists.

The Dedham Judgment

The conflict between liberals and conservatives was given further stimulus by a legal ruling arising from a dispute about the appointment of a new minister for the parish of Dedham, Massachusetts. To appreciate the significance of the Dedham Judgment, it is necessary to remember that in 1820, when it was delivered, Congregationalism still had the status of an established religion. In Massachusetts a parish consisted of all the male voters in the town. All paid the taxes, including a church tax. The church itself, however, was a smaller body within the parish. Generally it was this body that chose the minister, leaving the parish to ratify the appointment.

At Dedham, in 1818, two-thirds of the parish voted to select a liberal minister, Alvan Lamson, while a majority within the church wanted to appoint an orthodox candidate. The upshot was a secession of the church majority, who took with them the records and the communion plate. The minority remaining in the church then instituted legal proceedings for the recovery of the property. They were successful. The decision, upheld by the Supreme Judicial Court, was summarized in the Massachusetts reports: "When a majority of the members of a Congregational church separate from the majority of the parish, the members who remain, though a minority, constitute the Church in such a parish, and retain the rights and property belonging thereto." The Dedham Case thereafter served as a precedent for settling the affairs of divided congregations. Some parishes, however, became Unitarian without controversy.

The American Unitarian Association

During the first quarter of the nineteenth century there were several developments leading toward an embryonic denomination. The Society for Promoting Christian Knowledge, Piety and Charity was begun in

1806, and in 1816 the Evangelical Missionary Society, founded earlier in the century, broadened its basis and became distinctly Unitarian. In 1820 the first meeting of liberal ministers, the Berry Street Conference, was held in the Berry Street vestry of the Federal Street Church, Boston. A year later it adopted the name Ministerial Conference. The Publishing Fund Society was formed in 1821. From 1816 onwards the Unitarian position was strengthened at Harvard College. This led to the opening of Divinity Hall in 1826. Although many retained a preference for the term "Liberal," increasingly the younger ministers began to feel that "Unitarian" was the inevitable and most appropriate designation.

Divinity Hall, Harvard University

Because of this growing sense of Unitarian identity, those gathered at a meeting in the Federal Street Church vestry on 25 May 1825 – coincidentally, the same day as the meeting held in London to form the British and Foreign Unitarian Association – proposed to inaugurate an American Unitarian Association the following day. William Ellery Channing was elected president, but, as he was unable to accept because of ill health, the office fell to Aaron Bancroft. Ezra Stiles Gannett, one of the prime movers, was chosen secretary. Support for the American Unitarian Association was at first uncertain. Many liberals still felt the new departure too sectarian. Its usefulness was, however, confirmed as it responded to further revivals of orthodoxy.

21

The Transcendentalists

The controversy which had led to the separation of the Evangelical and Liberal streams of New England Congregationalism was hardly over before dissension broke out among Unitarians themselves, this time over the emergence of a new school of thought called Transcendentalism.

Transcendentalism is best understood in relation to the kind of Unitarianism it sought to counteract. The conflict was in part generational. Younger ministers began to find the older, rational Unitarianism of the Channing type inadequate. The religion of Channing's generation had been scriptural, ethical, and rational, but its engagement in controversy with the Evangelicals had given it a reputation for being negative. The Unitarian tendency to emphasize a rational approach to matters of faith had also made it, in the view of some, insensitive to the emotions. Now, under the influence of German philosophy and emerging Biblical criticism, new and broad questions were being asked, such as: What is religion about? The point at issue was whether religion, and specifically liberal religion, could ultimately be rational. The conventional answer had been emphatically yes. But the new school of thought began to suggest that religion was properly a matter of intuition, emotion, and faith.

Among the leading Transcendentalists were some of the greatest names in American literary history: Ralph Waldo Emerson, Henry David Thoreau, Theodore Parker, George Ripley, Bronson Alcott, Orestes Brownson, George Bancroft, and Margaret Fuller. Of the twenty-six members of the Transcendental Club, seventeen were Unitarian ministers. Geographically it was centered in Concord, Massachusetts.

It is not easy to define the beliefs that distinguished Transcendentalists from their more conservative – or, to be fair, their rather less radical – Unitarian contemporaries, not least because they themselves tended to resist codification. Indeed, it was the tendency to "transcend" this kind of formalization that gave them their name. Many were essentially pantheists. They saw and felt God everywhere, in all creation and especially in themselves. They ingested mysticism from Hindu and other Eastern scriptures, whose teaching of the immanence of the divine in the universe attracted them.

For a while the controversy threatened to divide the movement permanently. A few prominent Transcendentalists left the movement, but the majority remained Unitarian ministers. In time both parties were recognized as having contributed to what Unitarianism became.

The Miracles Controversy

While the Transcendentalist movement is generally remembered with reference to its leading figures – particularly Emerson, Thoreau and Parker – there were others who played significant roles in its origin. The first meeting of the Transcendental Club, in September 1836, took place at the home of George Ripley, the minister of Purchase Street Church, Boston. Two months later Ripley, an able student of German theology, wrote a review of James Martineau's *The Rationale of Religious Inquiry* for the *Christian Examiner*, highlighting how he had set aside miracles as proof of Christian teaching, and substituted intuition as the principal source of religious truth. As Parker would later do in his sermon on "The Transient and Permanent in Chris-

George Ripley

tianity," Ripley portrayed Christianity as a system of timeless religious and moral truths apprehended intuitively, rather than on the basis of miraculous evidence occurring in Biblical times.

Reaction to the review was led by Andrews Norton, Ripley's former teacher, and quickly developed into what has become known as the "miracles controversy." Norton, a scholar who had helped to establish the biblical case against the Trinity, had just spent fifteen years researching his monumental *Evidences of the Genuineness of the Gospels*, published in 1837, in which he argued that the miracles were the only incontrovertible evidence of the genuineness of the Christian revelation.

Thus, by 1836 the lines were already drawn for a conflict between the older and younger generations, which would publicly be ignited by a provocative graduation address two years later. Nor would it be without consequences for the harmony of ministerial and congregational relationships. Ripley, who was unable to interest his own congregation in the new ideas, resigned from his only ministerial charge in 1841 to take up the leadership of a communitarian experiment, based on the Associationist principles of the French utopian social theorist, Charles Fourier. The Brook Farm Institute of Agriculture and Education, in West Roxbury, Massachusetts, lasted until 1847.

Emerson's Divinity School Address

Ralph Waldo Emerson was the foremost moving spirit of the Transcendentalist movement. He held that having the emotions guided by the intellect had left Unitarianism without proper religious sensitivity, or, as he said, "corpse-cold." The son of the liberal minister William Emerson and a graduate of the Harvard Divinity School, he was, from 1829 to 1832,

Ralph Waldo Emerson

minister at Second Church, Boston. A disagreement with the congregation over his refusal to conduct communion services led to his resigning his pastoral charge. He nevertheless continued to preach in Unitarian churches until 1847, after which his connection with Unitarianism became nominal.

In 1833 Emerson visited Europe where he came under the influence of the Romantic Movement and German Idealism. New England Transcendentalism is but one example of how Western religious traditions became less cerebral and more experiential in the mid-nineteenth century. Emerson described how Transcendentalists viewed their cause: "There are always two parties, the party of the past and the party of the future; the establishment and the movement." Transcendentalists saw themselves as a movement, unfettered by the conservatism into which the previous generation had fallen. Arguably they were less than fair to those who sustain movements through organizations. They themselves exerted influence through the Transcendental Club. Emerson's own chief influence was through his published works: *The American Scholar* (1837), *Nature* (1838), several sets of essays, and, in particular, his Divinity School Address.

In 1838 Emerson was invited to give the valedictory address to the graduating students of the Harvard Divinity School. To the annoyance of the conservatives, he – unfairly, in their view – used the occasion to attack traditional supernaturalist Christianity. Beginning by stressing the importance of religious feeling and proclaiming that religion is not experienced second-hand, he then went on to argue that traditional Christianity enshrined two basic errors: its Christology, which emphasized miracles and the unique incarnation, and a false view of revelation as something that was only given in the past. The practical implications for the students were, he said, that they must cast conformity aside and acquaint people first hand with deity, and place all the emphasis on the inner experience of the soul.

The speech caused great offense. As soon as the Divinity School reopened after the recess, Henry Ware preached a sermon arguing the conservative case, in which he held that Emerson was denying the concept of a personal God, belittling Jesus, and rejecting the supernatural basis of Christianity. Some of Emerson's hearers, however, were deeply impressed. Among these was Theodore Parker.

Theodore Parker: The Transient and Permanent in Christianity

Theodore Parker, one of the younger ministers who heard Emerson's Divinity School Address, called it "the noblest, the most inspiring strain I ever listened to." It was Parker who gave popular currency to the debate over Transcendentalism. Described as "the Conscience of American Unitarianism," he was to have great influence on later developments, both in the United States and in Great Britain.

A grandson of Captain John Parker of Lexington, who in 1775, on the eve of the American Revolution, had declared, "If the British mean to have war, let it begin here," Theodore Parker was educated by private tutors. After teaching for a while, he entered Harvard Divinity School, where the influences of the time were the German theologians F. D. C. Schleiermacher, F. C. Baur and W. M. L. De Wette. In particular, Schleiermacher contended that religion was based on intuition and feeling, and independent of all dogma. He considered the highest religious experience to be a sensation of union with the infinite. Parker, taking up his first appointment as the minister of the First Parish of West Roxbury, promised his congregation, in the spirit of Schleiermacher and Emerson, "to preach nothing as religion that I have not experienced inwardly and made my own."

Theodore Parker

In 1841 Parker was invited to preach at the ordination and installation of Charles C. Shackford as minister of Hawes Place Church, South Boston. He took as his theme "The Transient and Permanent in Christianity." Like Channing's Baltimore manifesto, this sermon proved to be epoch-making. Taking the text, "Heaven and earth shall pass away, but my words shall not pass away" (Luke 21:33), he suggested that it indicated that Jesus believed that the religion he taught would be eternal. In Christianity, according to Parker, there were two elements: the one transient, the other permanent. He compared religion to physics: the solar system ever remains the same, while the models of Thales, Ptolemy, Copernicus, and Descartes are never final, but are only successive approximations to the truth. Likewise, the Christianity of Jesus is permanent, but what passes for Christianity in human society – popes, catechisms, sects, and churches – is transient. The teachings of Jesus are simple: absolute pure religion, absolute pure morality. No one can say his own notions will long stand, but all can say that the truth, as it is in Jesus, shall never pass away.

Not only did Parker give offense to the orthodox ministers who were present at the ordination of Shackford, but he alienated himself from most within the Unitarian movement. He was often oblivious to the effect that his words were capable of having on others. He failed to respond to the suggestions of his friends and supporters that this sometimes made him his own worst enemy. What most offended was his statement that "If it could be proved that Jesus of Nazareth had never lived, still Christianity would stand firm." He argued that Christianity shines by its own light and is its own evidence, and does not require miraculous support. As in the "miracles controversy" of 1836, the issue was essentially between those who clung to the "scriptural evidences" of supernatural religion and those who favored a natural religion that did not require miracles to support it.

Two years later, in 1843, Parker published his expanded and annotated lectures, which had originally been delivered in 1841 and 1842, as *Discourses on Matters Pertaining to Religion*. In 1844, having just returned from Europe, he took his turn preaching the traditional Thursday Lecture in the First Church, Boston. This address, "The Relation of Jesus to His Age and the Ages," resulted in further unpopularity. Unitarian ministers, most of whom had already barred him from their pulpits, now connived with the Boston Association of Ministers to exclude Parker from delivering future Thursday Lectures, by handing back the power of invitation to the minister of the First Church.

Despite being ostracized by his Unitarian colleagues, Parker was not without audiences. In 1846 he left West Roxbury to become minister to the 28th Congregational Society, which met in the Melodeon Theatre on Washington Street, Boston. This auditorium had seating for 2,700. Here he regularly preached to overflow audiences of more than 3,000, requiring removal to the larger Boston Music Hall in 1852. It was in this phase of his career that Parker became increasingly involved in radical social commitment, particularly the antislavery campaign.

Theodore Parker preaching at the Boston Music Hall

Some suggested that Parker had gone beyond a Christian position. It was anticipated that he would withdraw from the ministry. He refused to do so, however, and although there was little sympathy for his position, Unitarian ministerial associations could not bring themselves to expel him. The result was increasing bitterness over the Transcendentalist Controversy. Yet, for various reasons, no split ever developed between the Transcendentalists and the main Unitarian movement. This was partly because the Transcendentalists were indifferent to formal religion and organization, and partly a result of the Congregational principle, which prevented heresy hunts. Also not to be neglected was the fact that both radicals and conservatives found themselves diverted from sectarian theological disputes into common causes for social reform, such as the Ministry to the Poor, temperance, and the antislavery campaign.

"Parkerism" caused many to return to the fold of orthodoxy. Some have even suggested that in the period leading up to the American Civil War, American Unitarianism was at its lowest ebb. Not all historians agree. Some point out that the movement was extending its geographical reach beyond the New England heartlands. New churches were being gathered in Michigan, Iowa, Wisconsin, Kansas, Indiana, California and Canada. Moreover, to provide ministers for these societies, particularly those in the Mississippi basin, Meadville Theological School was established in 1844 at Meadville in western Pennsylvania. Many of the churches in the west, and the ministers who served them, were particularly receptive to Parker's ideas.

In 1860, in the last stages of tuberculosis, Parker visited Florence, Italy. There he died and is buried in the Protestant Cemetery. His popular advocacy of Transcendentalism and his radical social commitment had, on the eve of the Civil War, left the Unitarian movement deeply divided by controversy, but, nonetheless, geographically more widespread.

22

The Quest for Consensus

The Civil War

The Civil War brought together American Unitarians as nothing had previously done. At least sixty Unitarian ministers served in the field as chaplains, officers, enlisted men, or as members of the United States Sanitary Commission, which was organized and directed by Henry Whitney Bellows, minister of All Souls' Church, New York. Sanctioned by the government but independent of it, the Commission conducted a ministry to the sick and wounded. When its funds were exhausted in 1862, just prior to the Battle of Antietam, it received an unexpected gift of $100,000, raised in California by Thomas Starr King, the Unitarian minister in San Francisco. This gift was repeated two weeks later. King's

Civil War chaplains

1861 lecture campaigns throughout California won him the reputation of having saved California for the Union.

Starr King had originally been a Universalist minister, but was recruited for the Unitarians by Bellows. He had gone to California from Boston the year before the war began to organize a church. He died there at the age of only 39 years. In 1941 the Pacific School for the Ministry was renamed the Starr King School for the Ministry and is now associated with the University of California.

Henry W. Bellows and the National Conference

Believing that the Civil War had caused Americans to question their theological assumptions, Bellows thought that the postwar period would be a fruitful time for the expansion of Unitarianism. In his view, two things were holding Unitarianism back: internal dissension and the lack

of an effective nationwide organization. (The American Unitarian Association was then an organization of individuals, not congregations.) Bellows envisioned a broad church organization, non-sectarian in spirit, which would include not only avowed Unitarians, but also those who were tolerant and generous in their outlook. It was hoped it would attract the liberal element in all churches in America. To this end, Bellows persuaded the AUA to call a convention in New York City in April

Henry Whitney Bellows

1865. The outcome was a national conference of Unitarian churches, with each church or parish sending its minister and two lay delegates.

At the convention, there was extensive debate over whether the new organization, and by extension the Unitarian church generally, was a Christian organization. Bellows proposed calling it "The Liberal Christian Church of America." The convention eventually settled on "The National Conference of Unitarian Churches." As a gesture of reconciliation to the delegates who wanted a Christian basis, the convention adopted a constitution whose preamble referred to the Lord Jesus Christ and his kingdom.

The National Conference had little more ecumenical success than Martineau's Free Christian Union in Great Britain. Its breadth proved insufficient for some of the radicals, who suggested that the hint of sectarian narrowness in its organizational basis prevented members from consorting with freethinkers and Jews. It nonetheless had some success organizationally, raising money and stimulating the AUA, which began to organize churches in college towns.

James Freeman Clarke and the Battle of Syracuse

The issue of whether the National Conference was a Christian body was debated again at its next meeting, in Syracuse, New York, in 1866. James Freeman Clarke was the chief defender of the use of the term "Christian" in the organization's title and in the preamble to its constitution.

A grandson of James Freeman of King's Chapel, Clarke is now remembered for his famous "Five Points of Unitarianism," which were popular with Unitarian propagandists on both sides of the Atlantic at the beginning of the twentieth century. These points proclaimed that Unitarians believed in the Fatherhood of God, the Brotherhood of Man, the Leadership of Jesus, Salvation by Character, and "the progress of Mankind onward and upward for ever." Although this liberal optimism was severely undermined by the world wars of the twentieth century, Unitarians have tended to cling to it nevertheless.

An ally of the Transcendentalists, Clarke was tenacious in support of the Christian tradition. While he was prepared to interpret the term "Christian" broadly, he was unwilling to see it dropped altogether. The radicals' challenge was unsuccessful: the National Conference declined to revise its constitution, and even changed its name to the National Conference of Unitarian and Other Christian Churches.

James Freeman Clarke

O. B. Frothingham

W. J. Potter

The Free Religious Association

Feeling that their concerns were not being acknowledged by the National Conference, in 1867 the radicals broke away to form a new body, the Free Religious Association. Its aims were "to promote the interests of pure religion, to encourage the scientific study of theology, and to increase fellowship in the spirit." Its leaders were Octavius B. Frothingham and William J. Potter. Half of its 500 members, including Ralph Waldo Emerson, were or had been Unitarian ministers. While the new body did much to broaden Unitarian sympathies through its periodicals, *The Radical* (Boston, 1867-72) and *The Index* (New York, 1870-86), it made no attempt to organize churches. The Free Religious Association continued until well into the twentieth century and came to represent the Humanist position and the Ethical Culture movement.

Although most members of the Free Religious Association remained members of the National Conference as well, the denomination continued to be plagued by conflict between the more radical Unitarians and the more conservative. The conservatives' pulpits were closed to the radicals. Differences between the two parties led to the *Year Book* Controversy. For twenty-five years an annual *Year Book* had been published containing a list of Unitarian ministers and congregations. Although not an official publication, it served a useful purpose and broadly defined the Unitarian constituency. However, in 1873, the editor of the *Christian Register* invited those "who have ceased to accept Jesus as pre-eminently their spiritual leader" to withdraw from the Unitarian body. Frothingham, who presumably had not replied, asked why his name had been included, while Potter, who had responded, said that though theologically he was a Unitarian, he was not a Christian and left it to the editor to decide whether his name should, or should not, be included. In the end six names were dropped from the list. These were reinstated in 1884 with the approval of the AUA and the National Conference.

Jenkin Lloyd Jones and the Western Unitarian Conference

American Unitarianism had now expanded well beyond New England. Theological differences loomed even larger in the midwest, where the Western Unitarian Conference, formed in Cincinnati in 1852, coordinated churches west of the Alleghenies. Although at first fairly conservative, this area felt itself to be independent of New England. After the Civil War, a new generation of ministers encouraged greater theological diversity.

Among the new leaders was Jenkin Lloyd Jones, an immigrant from Cardiganshire, Wales, who had served in the Civil War. At the Meadville Theological Seminary he absorbed modern Biblical criticism, world religions, and evolution. Serving a church in Winnetka, Illinois, he quickly became one of the leaders of the Western Unitarian Conference. When the AUA tried to use its missionary funds to control the spread of radicalism in the west, Jones suggested that "It would be much better for the West

Jenkin Lloyd Jones

if the Association dropped [sending money] entirely and we were obliged to raise our missionary funds ourselves!" The Conference took up Jones's idea: in 1875, they decided to have no doctrinal test and, with their own funds, hired Jones to be their missionary. Until 1882, when he settled at a church in Chicago, Jones traveled extensively, supporting congregations throughout the west. He served on the board of the Western Unitarian Conference and edited its influential periodical, *Unity*. Jones and his co-editors, the "*Unity* men," were opposed to any sort of doctrinal statement. Rejecting traditional theological language, they emphasized "Freedom, Fellowship, and Character in Religion." Later on Jones, who helped to organize the 1893 World Parliament of Religions, became dissatisfied with his Unitarian colleagues' failure to share or commit to his interfaith ideals and declared his Chicago church undenominational. Late in life he further alienated himself from Unitarian organizations by opposing the American entry into World War I.

The Issue in the West

In 1884, Jones resigned as Secretary of the Western Unitarian Conference and was replaced by Jabez T. Sunderland. Sunderland, a Christian Unitarian, spoke for those who disagreed with the way the Western Unitarian Conference was moving away from the historic Christian roots of Unitarianism and who thought that lack of commitment to a definite platform was a weakness in extension work. In 1886, a week before a meeting of the Conference in Cincinnati, Ohio, he published a pamphlet, *The Issue in the West*, in which he warned that Unitarianism was doomed unless it stood for something more definite than ethical principles which it held in common with other churches and with secular society.

The Conference was in fact made up largely of theists and Christians. But even these felt that to make either Christianity or theism a condition of membership was to limit complete freedom of belief, which they regarded as a vital feature of their organization. At the Cincinnati meeting, Iowa City minister Oscar Clute proposed that "The primary object of this Conference is to diffuse the knowledge and promote the interests of pure Christianity." After this was resoundingly defeated, Sunderland offered a milder alternative, "that, while rejecting all creeds and creed limitations, the Conference hereby expresses its purpose as a body to be the promotion of a religion of love to God and love to man." This motion also failed. In the end, the Conference adopted, by a large majority, the following statement, proposed by one of the "*Unity* men," William Channing Gannett: "The Western Unitarian Conference conditions its fellowship on no dogmatic tests, but welcomes all who wish to join it to help establish Truth, Righteousness and Love in the world." Because this purely ethical statement disappointed the conservatives, Sunderland resigned his secretaryship and led a secession to form another body, the Western Unitarian Association. For a time it seemed that there might be two Unitarian organizations in the midwest.

There was widespread discussion of the "Issue in the West" throughout the American Unitarian constituency, and there were echoes of it in England, where it filled denominational periodicals even more than in America. Many observers maintained that the Western Unitarian Conference had adopted an atheistic and non-Christian basis.

William Channing Gannett, the son of AUA founder Ezra Stiles Gannett, and the principal opponent of Sunderland at the Cincinnati meeting, did not abandon the goal, which he shared with Sunderland, to find a statement that would encapsulate Unitarian theological consensus. At the 1887 meeting of the Western Unitarian Conference he proposed a new statement, "Things Most Commonly Believed To-day Among Us." "Above all doctrines," it read, "we emphasize the principles of freedom, fellowship, and character in religion. These principles make our all-sufficient test of fellowship." It noted that "specific statements of belief abound among us, always somewhat differing, always largely agreeing." Then it offered a sample credo, including belief in the Good, the authority of reason and conscience, the Bible and "all inspiring scriptures, old and new," "Jesus and all holy souls that have taught men truth and righteousness and love," "the growing nobility of man," a beautiful, orderly universe, the rewards of good and evil in life, working together to improve the world, and the overarching oneness of the divine. Although this statement was adopted by the Conference, it failed to immediately heal the breach. It was not until 1892, when Sunderland succeeded in attaching an amendment stating that the purpose of the Conference was to "promulgate a religion in harmony" with "Things Most Commonly Believed," that the controversy ended. By 1896 all the churches in the midwest were reunited within the Western Unitarian Conference.

The "Issue in the West" had an even more far-reaching result. In 1894 the National Conference revised the preamble to its constitution to satisfy both liberals and radicals. It read:

> These churches accept the religion of Jesus, holding, in accordance with his teaching, that practical religion is summed up in love to God and love to man. The Conference recognizes the fact that its constituency is Congregational in tradition and polity. Therefore, it declares that nothing in this constitution is to be construed as an authoritative test; and we cordially invite to our working fellowship any who, while differing from us in belief, are in general sympathy with our spirit and aims.

This preamble, unanimously adopted, proved acceptable to the Western Unitarian Conference as well and brought the midwesterners back into the national fold.

The National Conference eventually became the General Conference of the American Unitarian Association. In 1961, on the consolidation of the Unitarians and the Universalists, it was subsumed in the Unitarian Universalist Association. The Western Unitarian Conference, however, retained much of its organizational independence until the time of the consolidation. It did not contribute its money to the UUA, but instead created the Midwest Unitarian Universalist Foundation.

23

Twentieth-Century Renaissance

In the twentieth century, American Unitarianism made progress under the leadership of two Presidents of the American Unitarian Association sharing the surname of Eliot. (If there was a family relationship it had to have been a distant one.) Samuel A. Eliot's program had to contend with the exigencies of the United States' entry into World War I, while Frederick May Eliot faced corresponding difficulties during World War II. Yet each in his own way seized new opportunities afforded by the postwar world, just as Henry Bellows had done at the end of the Civil War.

Samuel A. Eliot

Under the administration of Samuel A. Eliot, elected in 1898, American Unitarians attempted to further extend their reach beyond their heartland in New England. When he was elected President in 1898 there were 457 Unitarian churches in North America, 301 of them in New England. Moreover, 204 of these were situated in small towns with populations of less than 10,000. According to Eliot, there was more potential for growth in suburbs and in college towns. He directed funds towards new churches and ministries that he thought would thrive and withheld money from older churches in poor and rural areas that could not be expected to pay back the loans. He claimed that he knew everyone on the list of ministers and the condition and prospect of every church.

The Unitarian Laymen's League was founded in 1907 to establish centers where Unitarian communities did not exist. In this task it met with a notable lack of success. It did, however resuscitate and reenergize a number of older churches. In 1919 it turned its attention to publicity. Within five years it had agents and offices in four cities, and 12,000 members. It held rallies, raised money, recruited ministers, helped to increase ministers' salaries, and developed advertising campaigns.

Samuel Atkins Eliot II

An advocate of national unity in the face of the crisis of World War I, Eliot had the AUA deny financial support to churches whose ministers opposed the war. The armistice in 1918 and the subsequent treaties set the stage for Unitarian participation in the field of international reconstruction, particularly in support of religious minorities, to which history had attuned Unitarian sensitivities. "We are," said Eliot, "creating a new internationalism." One immediate object of concern was the plight of the Unitarian community in Transylvania. British and American Unitarian commissions were sent to Transylvania between 1919 and 1927. A member of the American commission, Louis C. Cornish, wrote two reports, *Transylvania in 1922* (1923) and *The Religious Minorities in Transylvania* (1925). Unitarians responded to the situation with donations of money through the "sister church" program.

Eliot was a superb organizer who reformed the administration to strengthen the AUA at the center. He increased the size of the AUA staff, expanded the power of the executive, made its operations more business-like, developed a higher quality publication program, encouraged more professional ministry, and created departments of ministry and social justice. In 1927, when he resigned to return to the pastoral ministry at Arlington Street Church, Boston, he acknowledged, however, that his centralizing efforts had left the movement weak at its circumference.

New Theological Developments and the Humanist Manifesto

At this stage American Unitarian theology was predominantly theistic and Christian. Its essence is encapsulated in the catechism Eliot prepared for Unitarian Association Day in 1907. The minister asks: "What is the faith of our Unitarian churches?" The people reply: "These churches affirm the religion of Jesus, holding, in accordance with his teaching, that practical religion is summed up in love to God and love to man." Minister: "Why should we spread this gospel?" People: "To do our part in bringing in the Kingdom of God and to make truth and righteousness the foundation of the nation." A stout advocate of this liberal Christianity was Laurence

Sullivan. He had left the Roman Catholic Church in 1907, when priests and teachers were compelled to swear an anti-modernist oath. Besides holding several pastorates, Sullivan was mission preacher for the Unitarian Laymen's League.

Liberal Christianity generally, was, however, being challenged from without by the emergent neo-orthodoxy of Karl Barth, on the one hand, and, on the other, by the Process theology of Alfred North Whitehead and the naturalistic theology of Henry Nelson Wieman. Even more pressing was an assailant from within: religious humanism, which echoed the divisions previously expressed during the time of the Free Religious Association and the "Issue in the West." Moreover, the 1894 reconciliation between the AUA and the Western Unitarian Conference had the effect of giving the "ethically" based Unitarians a national voice.

Humanism was at first promoted through the ministries of isolated radicals, most of whom were converts from Baptist or Reformed churches. Then, in 1933, "A Humanist Manifesto" was published in the journal *The New Humanist*, and later in the *Christian Register*. The Manifesto asserted that the universe is self-existing and not created; that there are no supernatural or cosmic guarantees of human values; that nothing human is alien to the religious; and that the goal of humanism is a free and universal society in which people cooperate for the common good. There were only thirty-four signatories, all of them men and half of these Unitarian ministers. Whatever the Manifesto's eventual significance in the history of American Unitarianism, its publication, as humanist Lon Ray Call admitted, "fell like a dud in the battle-scarred career of American theological thought."

Louis C. Cornish

Following Samuel A. Eliot's mid-term resignation, Louis C. Cornish served as president of the AUA for a decade, continuing Eliot's policies. Cornish encouraged the continuing rapprochement with the Universalists. His main interest was in the expansion of international Unitarianism, particularly in the Philippines. Shortly after he entered office he came to believe that the Philippines' liberal Independent Church (Iglesia Filipina Independiente), formed in 1905 by the withdrawal of several millions from the Roman Catholic Church after Spain's defeat in the Spanish-American War, might become Unitarian. Unitarians became impatient with Cornish, however, when it became clear to them that his administration had failed to secure the affiliation with the Philippine Church. After the Second World

War the Independent Church affiliated with the Episcopal Church, where it found the traditions of liturgy and devotion more familiar.

"We content ourselves with exchanges of good will with a group of liberal Filipinos," wrote Kenneth McDougall, a lay member of the Wellesley Hills, Massachusetts, church, complaining of the administration's neglect of the denomination at home. "Neither today nor for several years past," he said, "have we . . . had a program worthy of our traditions and opportunities." He called for a "commission of appraisal."

Frederick May Eliot

It was for his part in the Commission of Appraisal that Frederick May Eliot came to embody the spirit of renewed enthusiasm for Unitarian renaissance and church extension. Eliot took office as president in 1937 and, echoing terminology used by Unitarian missionaries a century earlier, declared that it was time to adopt the adjective "aggressive" in thinking and talking about the denominational program – especially in the field of church extension.

The new administration applied itself most notably to Religious Education, to the work of the Unitarian Service Committee, and to strengthening regional organizations. The Commission had argued that church programs should be redefined in terms of education. This was put into practice by Ernest W. Kuebler, the director of religious education, and, with respect to children, by Sophia Lyon Fahs, who was responsible for the New Beacon Series of religious education publications, including the *Martin and Judy* books which presented religious issues within the everyday experience of children.

Frederick May Eliot

The Unitarian Service Committee (USC) grew out of a 1939 "service mission to Czechoslovakia." Martha and Waitstill Sharp were sent by the AUA to Prague to assist refugees from the Sudetenland and elsewhere to emigrate, and to rescue those facing Nazi persecution. The USC, organized the following year as a committee of the AUA, was to "investigate opportunities . . . for humanitarian service." During World War II, the Sharps and the USC, based in Lisbon and Marseilles, fed children in France, operated a medical clinic in Marseilles, and rescued more than 1,000 adults and children. After the war, the USC expanded its operations to nine European cities to aid the victims of the Nazis and other people displaced by the war. The USC's program for displaced children was taken over by the Universalist Service Committee, which was created in 1945. The assistance which the USC had

Unitarian Service Committee milk distribution center
Pau, France, 1940-1941

given to left-wing intellectual refugees came to haunt the Eliot administration when America entered the anti-Communist Cold War period.

As the once-independent *Christian Register* required increasing denominational subsidy, in 1939 the AUA took it over. It did not, nevertheless, lose its journalistic independence. Editor Stephen H. Fritchman gave increased attention to public issues, drawing criticism from those who thought that the official journal of the AUA was not a suitable organ for the discussion of politics. In May 1946, in the "witch-hunting" climate fostered by Congressional Committees on Un-American Activities, Fritchman was accused of being a Communist and of using the *Register* as pro-Soviet propaganda. A bitter conflict ensued. At first Eliot stood by Fritchman. When the editor refused to cooperate with the AUA board of directors, however, Eliot regretfully dismissed him. After leaving the *Register*, Fritchman served for twenty years as minister of the First Unitarian Church of Los Angeles.

Although only a few new churches were planted in the United States during the war, in 1944 the Church of the Larger Fellowship (CLF) was created to serve isolated Unitarians, out of reach of a local church, through the mail. Its Bond of Fellowship was "our earnest desire to lead pure, reverent, and useful lives, to seek together the love which quickens fellowship, and the truth which makes us free."

In 1947 the AUA created the Fellowship Office and appointed Monroe C. Husbands as its director. This office was to encourage the development of lay-led groups, or fellowships, in communities too small to support a church. The first fellowship was admitted in 1948. During the next decade more than three hundred others joined. Lon Ray Call, the founder of the movement, reported that, by 1967, eighty of these fellowships had become churches. Others chose to remain as they were, acknowledging the benefits of the "intimacy, spontaneity, informality" of do-it-yourself, lay-led groups.

During the postwar years the Beacon Press greatly expanded its operation and shifted from being a supplier of denominational tracts to being a general market publisher, albeit one with a liberal mission. A controversial book, Paul Blanshard's *American Freedom and Catholic Power* (1949) was its first bestseller. In 1955 Beacon Press pioneered the field of quality large-format paperbacks. Most significant of all was its publication in 1971 of the *Pentagon Papers*, documents about U.S. decision-making on Vietnam between 1940 and 1968, which exposed the disparity between secretive Government policy and the version presented to the public. As a result Beacon Press was subjected to a government campaign of intimidation, which only ended when the Watergate break-in drew the FBI's attention elsewhere. The director of Beacon Press at the time, Gobin Stair, called the publication "a watershed event in the denomination's history and a high point in Beacon's fulfilling its role as a public pulpit for proclaiming Unitarian Universalist principles.

Consolidation with the Universalists

Frederick May Eliot died in office in 1958 at the age of sixty-eight, three years before his term as President was to have expired. He had achieved much, but the consolidation of the AUA with the Universalist Church of America remained to be completed. From the 1950s onwards, some activities of the two denominations had been combined, including the merger of the of the youth organizations, American Unitarian Youth and the Universalist Youth Fellowship, to create Liberal Religious Youth. Moreover, in 1953 the denominations came together in a Council of Liberal

Churches (Unitarian-Universalist) for the purposes of religious education, publications, and public relations. With discussions for union underway, and because of uncertainties concerning the outcome, the board of directors of the AUA nominated Ernest W. Kuebler to succeed Eliot, believing his proven administrative ability would ensure continuity. The election was, however, successfully contested by Dana McLean Greeley, who was nominated by petition. Greeley served as last president of the AUA.

The plan for consolidation was presented to a joint meeting of the two denominations at Syracuse, New York, 29-31 October 1959. A major problem discussed was how to do justice to the continuity of Unitarianism with its Christian roots, while also acknowledging the universal nature of religious truth. That this echoed the so-called "Battle of Syracuse" in 1866, in the same city, was not lost on those attending.

Finally, after three days, the two parties agreed "To cherish and spread the universal truths taught by the great prophets and teachers of humanity in every age and tradition, immemorially summarized in the Judeo-Christian heritage as love to God and love to man." The plan was then ratified at simultaneous meetings held in Boston on 23 May 1960. Legal steps to consolidate were completed in May 1961. The achievement was celebrated at a joint service with the singing of Marion Franklin Ham's hymn:

> As tranquil streams that meet and merge
> And flow as one to seek the sea,
> Our kined fellowships unite
> To build a church that shall be free.

24

American Universalism

A detailed history of the Universalist movement and the Universalist Church of America is beyond the scope of this volume. A brief outline is, however, necessary to understand present day Unitarian Universalism.

The values shared by Unitarians and Universalists, celebrated at the time of their 1961 consolidation and since, have tended to obscure their separate and distinctive origins. From their beginnings, each had an aversion to Calvinism. Their adherents, who belonged to different socioeconomic strata, had expressed this antipathy in different ways. Moreover, while the Unitarian movement was an attempt at the liberalization of established church order from within, the Universalists were a direct challenge to it.

Class differences, in the early stages, are illustrated by the reluctance of the Arminian, Charles Chauncy, to publish his treatise on universal salvation, *The Mystery Hid from Ages and Generations* (eventually published anonymously in 1784), for fear of being associated with John Murray, one of the founding fathers of American Universalism. Murray's universalism was fundamentally predestinarian, rather than Arminian: he had simply broadened the category of the elect to embrace all of humankind. Far from regarding Murray as part of a liberal crusade against Calvinism, Chauncy saw him as a revivalist rabble-rouser who preached an odd version of the emotional religion to which he and the other liberals were opposed.

There were foreshadowings of Universalism in America during the seventeenth century. In 1636 Sir Henry Vane the Younger, a liberal governor of Massachusetts, later beheaded in England for his political opinions, "began to broach new tenets," which may have included that of universal salvation, belief in which is evident in his later writings. The following year Samuel Gorton, the founder of a colony that later became part of Rhode

Island, affirmed that "There is no heaven but in the hearts of men, no hell but in the mind." In 1684, Joseph Gatchell of Marblehead, Massachusetts had his tongue pierced by order of the Suffolk County Court, for saying, "All men should be saved."

The doctrine of universal salvation was widespread among the German mystical pietists who sought refuge from persecution by settling in Pennsylvania: Dunkers, Huguenots, Moravians, and Mennonites. Dr. George de Benneville, a medical practitioner born in London of French parents, who had already undertaken missions to Germany, Holland, and Italy, settled among these German immigrants in 1741 and preached that all will be finally redeemed by the love of God.

The arrival of John Murray from England, in 1770, provided the major thrust toward an organized Universalist movement. Murray, who had been a class leader at George Whitefield's Methodist Tabernacle in London, was converted to the views of the English Universalist James Relly, who believed that a mystical union between Christ and all of humanity conferred the benefits of salvation upon all. Following the death of his wife and child, Murray sailed for a new life in America. He then had no thoughts of any further religious career. Fortuitously landing at Good Luck Bay, New Jersey, he met Thomas Potter, who persuaded him to preach in a meetinghouse he had erected on his farm. Convinced that these circumstances were a sign from God, Murray began a wide-ranging itinerant preaching career.

John Murray

A few years later Murray was invited to preach to a group of people in Gloucester, Massachusetts, who had been studying Relly's *Union* (1759). In 1779, with Murray as their minister, they seceded from the First Parish Church to create an Independent Church of Christ. In its articles of association the congregation agreed "To be bound together by . . . Christ's love; to acknowledge no master but Jesus Christ; to follow no guide in spiritual matters but His word and His spirit, and no more to be entangled by any yoke of bondage." On Christmas Day, 1780, they dedicated a church building and ordained their minister. In 1786, after protracted legal proceedings, Universalists were allowed to use their parish taxes to support their own church. Soon afterward Murray won the right of Universalist clergy to be recognized as ordained ministers with power to perform marriage ceremonies. In 1793 Murray left Gloucester to settle with the First Universalist Society of Boston.

Equally important, at this stage, was the influence of Caleb Rich and other American-born evangelists operating in rural New England. Between 1773 and 1778, Rich had a series of visionary experiences which first convinced him that none would be everlastingly damned, and later that all would, in spirit, rejoin God after death. In 1775, partway along this religious road, and while on leave from the American Revolutionary Army, he, together with some like-minded cousins, evangelized in the area of Oxford, Massachusetts, near where Rich had been born. This activity, and the work of Rich's early colleagues, Adams Streeter and Thomas Barns, led to the formation of the earliest Universalist societies outside of Murray's orbit: in Warwick, Oxford, and Milford, Massachusetts. Rich's experience of ecstatic conversion suggests that many early Universalists shared the evangelical sensibilities that had first emerged in the Great Awakening and which resurfaced in subsequent waves of revivalism.

In 1781 Elhanan Winchester, a Calvinist Baptist minister who had come to believe in universal salvation, was expelled from his church in Philadelphia for heresy. He then organized members from his former congregation as the Society of Universal Baptists. Unlike Relly and Murray, who believed that all were saved immediately after death (though they might remain miserable until themselves reconciled to God), Winchester, like Chauncy, maintained that for hardened sinners there was a remedial period of punishment or discipline, perhaps lasting tens of thousands of years. In 1787 Winchester sailed for Great Britain, where during seven years of missionary activity he launched small Universalist movements in

Elhanan Winchester

England and Scotland, and, in 1788, published *Dialogues on Universal Salvation*. While he was away from America, in 1790 the Philadelphia Convention was organized at his church to unite the Universalist societies throughout Pennsylvania, New Jersey, and New England "in one General Church in bands of love and uniformity." This organization, at which New England Universalists were little represented (usually only by Murray), remained in existence for over a decade.

A more long-lasting organization, the New England Universalist General Convention (founded in 1793), meeting at Winchester, New Hampshire in 1803, adopted a statement of belief, since known as the Winchester Profession of Faith, which illustrates the early movement's unequivocal biblical stance:

> We believe that the Holy Scriptures of the Old and New Testament contain a revelation of the character of God, and of the duty, interest and final destination of mankind; we believe that holiness and true happiness are inseparably connected, and that believers ought to be careful to maintain order and practice Good Works, for these things are good and profitable unto men; we believe that there is one God, whose nature is Love, revealed in one Lord Jesus Christ, by one Holy Spirit of Grace, who will finally restore the whole family of mankind to holiness and happiness.

Lest it be thought that the Profession might seem too much like a creed, the Convention also adopted the following liberty clause:

> Yet while we adopt a general profession of belief ... we leave it to the several churches, societies or to smaller associations of churches, if such should be formed, within the limits of our General Association to continue or adopt within themselves, such more articles of faith ... as may appear to them best under their particular circumstances, provided they do not disagree with our general profession or plan.

Hosea Ballou's Theological Innovations

The initial phase of the Universalist movement, rooted in emotionalism, was soon modified, in the early 1800s, under the leadership of Hosea Ballou. The new departure did not altogether erase the evangelical piety, but its dominant emphasis was a rationalism that gave it a greater affinity with Unitarianism. The shift in Ballou's thinking, begun around 1795, was cast in largely complete form a decade later in his influential *Treatise on Atonement* (1805). Ballou was the youngest of eleven children of a New Hampshire farmer who was also a Baptist lay preacher. As a teenager he encountered the ideas of Caleb Rich and other itinerant Universalist preachers. He became a Universalist minister himself in 1794, eventually settling at the Second Universalist Church in Boston.

Hosea Ballou

Ballou's major purpose in the *Treatise on Atonement* was "to prove the doctrine of universal holiness and happiness" and to demonstrate by the application of reason and the examination of the scriptures, the falsity of "the idea that sin is infinite, and that it deserves infinite punishment; that the law transgressed is infinite and inflicts an infinite penalty; and that the great Jehovah took on himself a natural body of flesh and blood, and actually suffered death on a cross, to satisfy his infinite justice, and thereby save his creatures from endless misery." The aim was to prove that God was not a wrathful deity seeking justice, but a benevolent being full of infinite love. Jesus was sent to earth not to atone for human sin, but to lead people to divine love. He had suffered for men, not instead of them. Thus, Ballou rejected the traditional doctrine of vicarious atonement. The love of God was not reserved for a few, as the doctrine of predestination implied. Here was a clear and logical exposition of universal salvation.

Though secondary to his main purpose, Ballou had also rejected as unscriptural and irrational the doctrines of the trinity, the fall, human depravity, and salvation by faith alone. Moreover, he went on to affirm "the unchanging love of God as the supreme trait in Godhead; his eternal Fatherhood; Man's sonship to God; Jesus as the reconciler of Man to God; the certainty of punishment for Sin, and the final salvation of all souls."

Ballou believed that sins were punishable on earth and not in any other state: heaven, hell, purgatory, or otherwise. The question of "future punishment" for sin divided early nineteenth-century Universalists, leading to the secession of a minority, known as Restorationists, who did not share Ballou's views and could not be reconciled to his outspoken promotion of them in denominational circles. The Restorationists argued that sentiments of "no future accountability" were subversive of the best interests of society. During the 1830s they met separately as the Massachusetts Association of Universal Restorationists, developing a rapprochement with the Unitarians, which paved the way for even closer ties as the century progressed. When the Restorationists ceased to meet as a separate denomination, most of the ministers remained with the Unitarian churches they had come to serve. Meanwhile, as Ballou's personal influence waned, a more moderate advocacy of future punishment was established as the Universalist norm. In 1878 the Universalist ministers of Boston issued a statement, saying, "We believe that repentance and salvation are not limited to this life." By this time American Universalists were almost unanimously Restorationist in belief.

A lesser stir was caused in the 1840s by arguments over Universalist commitment to the inerrancy of the Biblical revelation and the evidential relevance of the miracles. At this stage, however, the denomination remained overwhelmingly committed to its Christian expressions, as is suggested by the adoption of an official seal in 1866, which bore the device of a Bible surmounted by a cross, over which was emblazoned the legend, "Christ will Conquer."

Organization

In the early 1830s the New England General Convention was reorganized as the Universalist General Convention, the official governing body of all Universalist churches in the United States. In 1899 the Convention approved the following Essential Principles of the Universalist Church: "The Universal Fatherhood of God; the spiritual authority and leadership of His Son Jesus Christ; the trustworthiness of the Bible as containing a revelation from God; the certainty of just retribution for sin, and the final harmony of all souls with God."

Nineteenth-century social reform movements both attracted and divided the Universalists, some of whom were ardent advocates of temperance, abolition, workers' and women's rights. Some who had been Universalist ministers went on to pursue communitarian experiments. In 1839 Abner Kneeland, who had been expelled from the Universalists for "infidelity" and who had been convicted of blasphemy by a Massachusetts court, founded a settlement called Salubria in Iowa, a community of families living as farmers and using their leisure time to study social and religious questions. It survived only until the death of Kneeland in 1844. Of longer duration was the Restorationist Adin Ballou's socialist, pacifist, and utopian community in Hopedale, Massachusetts, which lasted from 1841 until 1856.

Universalists were strong advocates of education. Twenty secondary schools were founded by Universalists during the nineteenth century, beginning with Nichols' Academy at Dudley, Massachusetts, in 1819. Universalists established five colleges, including Lombard College, 1851, in Galesburg, Illinois (now incorporated in Meadville/Lombard Theological School, a graduate theological college associated with the University of Chicago); Tufts University, 1852, in Medford, Massachusetts; and St. Lawrence University, 1856, in Canton, New York.

Olympia Brown

Tufts's charter enshrined its liberal ethos: "No instructor in the said College shall ever be required by the masters to profess any particular religious opinions as a test of office, and no student shall be refused admission to or denied any of the privileges, honors, or degrees of the said College, on account of the religious opinions he may entertain." Nor was entry into the ministry confined to men. In 1863 Universalists ordained Olympia Brown. Other women ministers soon followed.

To the distress of many Universalists, the Tufts and St. Lawrence theological schools ceased to exist after the Unitarian Universalist consolidation. Their resources were, nonetheless, applied in favor of Unitarian Universalist ministerial training.

A New Identity

Clarence R. Skinner, the leading Universalist theologian of the early twentieth century, adapted the Christian Social Gospel movement to Universalism, envisioning the church as a way to use religious teachings to help those in need and to address injustice. He wrote "A Declaration of Social Principles" which was approved by the denomination in 1917. In it he wrote, "We hold it to be self-evident that mankind is led into sin by evil surroundings, by the evils of unjust social and economic conditions, which condemn one to be born in the squalor and filth of the slums, and another admidst the equally demoralizing influences of unearned luxury." He called for democracy as both "an inherent right" and a "divinely imposed duty," equal participation by women in all affairs of life, government control of essential industries, a guaranteed standard of living for all by social insurance, and an end to war. He thought it impossible for anyone to live a fully Christian life in an unchristian social order. Therefore it was the job of the church to "to educate and inspire the community and the nation to a keener social consciousness and a truer vision of the kingdom of God on the earth."

Skinner's congregation, the Community Church of Boston, was dedicated to "the study of universal religion." This understanding of Universalism as not merely Christianity, but as a faith encompassing all the world's religions, was developed further following World War II. Though this disturbed the more conservative Christian wing of the denomination, many believed that it was a logical development. In 1947 the General Superintendent, Robert Cummins, suggested that "a circumscribed Universalism is unthinkable." Two years later Brainard Gibbons, who would succeed Cummins as General Superintendent in 1953, asked, "Is Universalism a Christian denomination, or is it something more, a truly universal religion?" The major force for change came from a group of recently qualified ministers from Tufts's Crane Theological School who called themselves the Humiliati (humble ones). Given to liturgical innovation, the group adopted as a symbol an off-center cross enclosed by a circle, to illustrate that while Universalism recognized its Christian roots, Christianity was no longer necessarily central to the faith.

These liturgical innovations took their most extreme form in the newly founded Charles Street Meeting House, Boston, where the Unitarian minister Kenneth L. Patton adorned the sanctuary with symbols of the world's faiths. Pews were arranged in the round and focused on a mural of the nebula in Andromeda. The congregation was never large, but Patton's talented liturgical writing had wide influence on both Universalists and Unitarians.

The change from Christian to "universalized Universalism" gradually became institutionalized. This was how the movement's leaders presented their faith as they moved towards the 1961 consolidation with the Unitarians. There remained many, of course, who held to older interpretations of what Universalism meant.

The changing face of American Universalism, 1870s to 1950s
The off-center cross symbol indicated that Christianity was no longer
regarded as central to Universalist identity

25

Unitarian Universalism

In the wake of the 1961 Unitarian Universalist consolidation, it took some time to achieve rationalization of the two denominations' administrative and organizational structures. The *Universalist Leader* and the *Christian Register* were immediately combined into the *Register-Leader*, the forerunner of the *UU World*. The two ministerial associations were amalgamated in 1961, as were the two Churches of the Larger Fellowship, catering for those beyond the reach of regular congregations. The two Service Committees came together in 1963, followed by the creation of the Unitarian Universalist Women's Federation from the former Association of Universalist Women and the Unitarian Women's Alliance. The denominational historical societies, more deeply attached to historic sensibilities, remained separate until 1978, when they finally came together as the Unitarian Universalist Historical Society.

Care was taken to establish confidence that the traditions of one body would not be submerged in those of the other. Universalists in particular were afraid that they might be the losers in this respect, and perhaps not without reason when it came to questions of leadership and ministerial education. They would have preferred that neither the last president of the American Unitarian Association, Dana McLean Greeley, nor the last General Superintendent of the Universalist Church of America, Philip Randall Giles, be eligible for election as president of the merged body. Greeley, however, was the choice of the nominating committee. William Rice, another Unitarian, who had been chair of the Joint Commission on Merger, was nominated by petition. Greeley carried the day by 1,135 votes to 980. To secure balance, care had to be taken over further appointments. Accordingly Raymond Hopkins, a Universalist, was elected as executive vice-president.

The combining of the consolidated denominations' ministerial education programs also dealt the Universalists some painful blows. In order to
cut costs and centralize the provision of theological education, the UUA
recommended closing the Universalist seminaries at Tufts University
(Crane Theological School) and at St. Lawrence University (Canton Theological School). In future, Unitarian Universalist ministerial preparation
would be almost entirely at Meadville/Lombard Theological School in
Chicago – itself the product of a 1928 merger between the Universalist
Ryder Divinity School at Lombard College and the Unitarian Meadville
Theological School – and at Starr King School for the Ministry in Berkeley,
California, as well as at Harvard Divinity School. Starr King was a Unitarian seminary, and Harvard, though independent, had a long tradition
of association with the Unitarians.

The real or supposed dominance of the Unitarians was also reflected
in the insensitivity of some who referred to Unitarian Universalists simply
as "Unitarians," a misdemeanor for which fines were imposed at meetings
of the Unitarian Universalist Association's Board of Trustees. The publication in 1970 of George Huntston Williams's *American Universalism: A
Bicentenary Essay*, to mark the two hundredth anniversary of John Murray's
meeting with Thomas Potter, did much to increase Unitarian appreciation
of Universalist traditions.

Some on both sides, including the Unitarian A. Powell Davies, minister
of All Souls' Church, Washington, who regarded the Universalists as too
conservative, had resisted merger. In the end, nearly all churches of both
denominations consented to the new arrangement, the exceptions being
a few Universalist churches in the Deep South.

With the administrative problems resolved and their constituencies in
the process of adjusting to the new situation, Unitarian Universalists gave
their attention to clarifying and presenting the principles that bound them
together. In 1985 the Association adopted the following statement:

> We, the member congregations of the Unitarian Universalist Association,
> covenant to affirm and promote
> • The inherent worth and dignity of every person;
> • Justice, equity and compassion in human relations;
> • Acceptance of one another and encouragement to spiritual growth in
> our congregations;
> • Free and responsible search for truth and meaning;

- The right of conscience and the use of the democratic process within our congregations and in society at large;
- The goal of world community with peace, liberty, and justice for all;
- Respect for the interdependent web of all existence of which we are a part.

The living tradition which we share draws from many sources:

- Direct experience of that transcending mystery and wonder, affirmed in all cultures, which moves us to a renewal of the spirit and an openness to the forces which create and uphold life;
- Words and deeds of prophetic women and men which challenge us to confront powers and structures of evil with justice, compassion, and the transforming power of love;
- Wisdom from the world's religions which inspires us in our ethical and spiritual life;
- Jewish and Christian teachings which call us to respond to God's love by loving our neighbors as ourselves;
- Humanist teachings which counsel us to heed the guidance of reason and the results of science, and warn us against idolatries of the mind and spirit.

Grateful for the religious pluralism which enriches and ennobles our faith, we are inspired to deepen our understanding and expand our vision. As free congregations we enter into this covenant, promising to one another our mutual trust and support.

To this, in 1993, a sixth clause was added acknowledging the development of environmental issues and their attendant spiritualities:

- Spiritual teachings of earth-centered traditions which celebrate the sacred circle of life and instruct us to live in harmony with the rhythms of nature.

25 Beacon Street, Boston
Headquarters of the Unitarian Universalist Association

PART 4

A GLOBAL RELIGION

26

Unitarianism in Asia and Africa

The emergence of Unitarianism as a global religion has never been a matter of spreading the faith from a central source. Indeed, efforts by foreign missionaries to spread Unitarianism in Asia have not met with much success. The American Unitarian Association supported a mission in Japan from the 1890s to the 1920s, but was not able to establish a self-sustaining church. In the Philippines, despite the efforts of AUA president Louis Cornish, the Philippine National Church ultimately chose to affiliate with the Anglicans rather than with the Unitarians. The present-day Unitarian Universalist Church of the Philippines is the descendant of an indigenous Universalist group founded in the 1950s by the Rev. Toribio S. Quimada.

Beginning in the late eighteenth century, indigenous Unitarian movements have arisen within Christian communities in various places in Asia (particularly India) and in Africa. Like their counterparts in Britain and America, these Unitarian movements developed in response to local conditions. Often, their founders arrived at their ideas independently and only later discovered that there were other people who thought as they did.

Over the years, when Unitarians from different backgrounds encountered each other, they have recognized each other as kindred spirits. Antitrinitarian Dissenters in Britain understood that they had something in common with European Socinians. American Arminians, somewhat reluctantly, acknowledged their kinship with British Unitarians. The same thing has happened in more recent times in Asia and Africa. Spencer Lavan called the history of Unitarianism in India a story of people "on three different continents who unexpectedly discovered that they had much in common and much worth sharing."

The Unitarian Christian Church of Madras

The story of Unitarianism in India begins with William Roberts (1768-1838), a Tamil from the area around Madras (present-day Chennai). Born Thiruvenkatam Vellala in war-torn south India, he was sold into slavery as a youth and ended up as the personal servant of an English sea captain. Accompanying his employer's family to Europe, in 1789 he converted to Christianity and was baptized an Anglican, taking the baptismal name of William Roberts. He diligently studied the Bible and the Book of Common Prayer, but was troubled by the Athanasian Creed. "Three persons of the same power and attributes," he later wrote, "each separately God and Lord, yet altogether no more than one God, was a thing too hard for me to make anything of." On a second trip to England in 1793, Roberts discovered Unitarianism when a fellow servant introduced him to the writings of Joseph Priestley and Theophilus Lindsey. The next year, he returned to India, bringing a collection of Unitarian books.

The Unitarian Christian Church of Madras dates its origin to 1795, when Roberts gathered a small group of ten families for Unitarian services, using a Tamil translation of Lindsey's *Reformed Prayer Book*. Feeling a need for professional religious leadership, in 1816 Roberts wrote to the Unitarian Society for Promoting Christian Knowledge in London, requesting them to send a missionary. Although this request was denied, over the years British Unitarians have provided encouragement, Unitarian publications, and a modest amount of financial support. The church has always been small and poor, but it has survived, celebrating its two hundredth anniversary in 1995. Today the church has over 200 members, still worshipping in the chapel built by Roberts in 1813. With the help of Partner Churches in Edinburgh and Glasgow, it maintains two schools, one in Chennai and one in the Dalit ("untouchable") village of Ammanabakkum.

Unitarians in Calcutta and the Brahmo Samaj

Unitarianism in Calcutta begins with William Adam, a Baptist missionary who converted to Unitarianism while working on a translation of the New Testament into Bengali in 1821. Expelled by the Baptists, Adam formed a committee to organize Unitarianism in Calcutta.

Adam's partner in the translation project was Rammohun Roy, a liberal reformer in the Hindu tradition. Impressed by Rammohun's program of strict monotheism, liberal social reform, interfaith dialogue, and the use of reason in religion, Adam described him to British and American Unitarians as a "Unitarian Hindu." Since Rammohun admired the ethical teachings of Jesus, and provided financial support to the Unitarian mission, Adam and the Unitarians tended to claim him as one of their own. Rammohun, however, wanted to reform his cultural heritage, not to reject it. In 1828 he founded a liberal Hindu organization, the Brahmo Samaj (Society of God).

In 1854, an American Unitarian, Charles Timothy Brooks, visited India and returned enthusiastic about the prospects for a Unitarian mission. The following year, the American Unitarian Association sent Charles Dall to Calcutta as missionary and minister of the Unitarian church. He remained in Calcutta for 31 years, but had limited success as a missionary. As William Adam had discovered a generation before, Dall found that while liberal Hindus, and some Muslims, were interested in learning about Unitarian Christianity and Transcendentalism, and even willing to support the mission, few were interested in converting. In the end, it was Dall who converted. He became a supporter of Indian nationalism, comparing the British rule in India to American slavery. In 1871 he became the first Christian, and the first non-Indian, to join the Brahmo Samaj.

The Brahmo Samaj continues today as a distinct, liberal and tolerant faith with fifty samajes throughout India. The relationship between Brahmos and Unitarians continues through their membership in the International Association for Religious Freedom.

Unitarianism in the Khasi and Jaintia Hills

In 1887 Jabez Sunderland, the Unitarian minister in Ann Arbor, Michigan and editor of *The Unitarian*, received a letter from Hajjom Kissor Singh, a 22-year-old from the Khasi Hills in northeastern India. The Khasis, a tribal people originally from southeast Asia, had been largely converted to Christianity a generation before by Welsh Calvinist missionaries. Like British and American Unitarians before him, Singh came to Unitarianism by questioning Calvinist doctrine. As a teenager, he had developed his own form of Christianity,

Hajjom Kissor Singh

which he called "The Religion of One God." A sympathetic Brahmo told him that his religion sounded like Unitarianism, and put him in touch with Charles Dall. After reading the writings of William Ellery Channing, particularly the sermon "Unitarian Christianity Most Favorable to Piety," Singh decided that he was indeed a Unitarian and set out to organize a Unitarian church.

In 1895, while on sabbatical from Ann Arbor, Sunderland went to India as representative of the British and Foreign Unitarian Association. In Madras he met William Roberts's son, still faithfully tending the "forlorn" Unitarian church, and still hoping for a foreign missionary. In Calcutta he facilitated a reconciliation between rival branches of the Brahmo Samaj. In the new spirit of interfaith dialogue fostered by the 1893 World Parliament of Religions, he helped the Unitarians and the Brahmos explore ways to cooperate without trying to convert each other. Like Charles Dall, he supported Indian nationalism, and wrote an influential article on the subject in the *Atlantic Monthly*. In the Khasi Hills, he ordained David Edwards, a Khasi Unitarian converted from Methodism.

Although the Khasi Unitarians were few – about 60 people in four small congregations – Sunderland was impressed by their dedication and their steadfastness in the face of persecution. He urged British and American Unitarians to assist them. The British Unitarians, who had declined to send missionaries to Madras, did send ministers, as well as financial support and publications to the Khasi Hills. With support from British, American, and Canadian Unitarians, Margaret Barr served the region for 37 years, from 1936 until her death in 1973. In addition to ministry, she founded nonsectarian schools and helped to organize medical care, water supply, and sanitation.

Today the Khasi Unitarian Union is the largest Unitarian group in Asia, with over 9,000 members in more than thirty congregations.

Margaret Barr

Unitarianism in South Africa

The person considered the founder of Unitarianism in South Africa, the Rev. Dawid Faure, was not himself a Unitarian. He was a South African who went to the Netherlands to study for the ministry of the Dutch Reformed Church. While at the University of Leiden, he adopted liberal views. On his return to South Africa in 1867, he organized a liberal Christian congregation, the Free Protestant Church of Cape Town. His message, which he called simply "the new theology," was that human beings are capable of choosing good as well as evil, and that the human race has the potential for gradual moral and spiritual improvement. He emphasized the use of reason and denied the doctrines of original sin, human depravity, predestination, and eternal punishment.

The minister of the Free Protestant Church from 1897 to 1937 was Ramsden Balmforth, a Unitarian from England. During his tenure, the church affiliated with the General Assembly of Unitarian and Free Christian Churches in Britain. For the next forty years, it was served by Unitarian and Unitarian Universalist ministers from Britain and the United States.

In 1977 Robert Steyn became the church's first South African minister since Dawid Faure. After Steyn died in 1997, Gordon Oliver, a social activist and former mayor of Cape Town, stepped in as lay minister and was ordained in 2002. There are currently four Unitarian congregations in South Africa. They recently established a national organization.

Unitarianism in Nigeria

The Unitarian churches of Nigeria trace their origin to Dr. Adeniran Adedeji Ishola. Originally an Anglican, he left the church in 1918 to found a group called "First Free Thinkers" which combined liberal Christianity with elements of the Yoruba indigenous tradition. In 1921 they changed their name to the Unitarian Brotherhood Church, after Ishola found the word "Unitarian" in a dictionary and decided that it described their beliefs. Despite persecution – Dr. Ishola was arrested on a charge of disturbing the peace, lost his job, and survived an attempt on his life – the church persevered and grew.

The Unitarian Brotherhood Church was a pioneer in introducing African cultural practices into Christian worship. Services are held in the Yoruba language, children are baptized with Yoruba names, and the services include drumming and other African music.

The First Unitarian Church of Nigeria, a new Unitarian church, with more of an emphasis on social activism, was formed in 1994.

Emerging Unitarian Movements

Unitarianism continues to be rediscovered in our time. Perhaps because the development of the Internet has facilitated communication across vast distances of space and culture, the 1990s and 2000s have been particularly rich years for the emergence of new Unitarian communities.

There are approximately one hundred Unitarian Universalist Christians in Pakistan, led by Inderias Dominic Bhatti, who discovered Unitarian Universalism in 1991. Like Hajjom Kissor Singh and Adeniran Adedeji Ishola, Bhatti developed his own liberal religious ideas and later discovered that they were similar to ideas held by Unitarian Universalists. Similarly, Fulgence Ndagijimana of Burundi discovered Unitarianism via an Internet search in 2003. With assistance from Unitarians in Britain, he organized L'Assemblée des chrétiens unitariens de Burundi as "a community within which differences are viewed as a richness and spiritual search is limited only by the finite capacity of the human mind."

There are emerging Unitarian and Unitarian Universalist groups in Sri Lanka, Congo, Cuba, Mexico, and Indonesia. In Indonesia, Unitari-

ICUU African Leadership Conference
Nairobi, Kenya, 2008

anism developed out of the Seventh Day Adventist tradition; Unitarians there celebrate the Sabbath beginning on Friday at sunset, and hold their services on Saturday.

New Unitarian groups such as these, often living in conditions of great hardship, poverty, and sometimes persecution, benefit from the ideas, experience, and material assistance of those in easier circumstances. In turn, these new communities make an important contribution to worldwide Unitarianism. Their faithfulness and dedication in the face of adversity is a powerful witness to the continuing vitality, importance, and relevance of the Unitarian message.

Appendix

A Bibliographical Essay
References and Further Reading

The major sources used for the preparation of this book were Earl Morse Wilbur's *Our Unitarian Heritage* (Beacon Press, 1925); his later monumental two-volume *History of Unitarianism: Vol. 1, Socinianism and its Antecedents* (Harvard University Press, 1947) and *Vol. 2, In Transylvania, England and America* (Harvard University Press, 1952); and George Huntston Williams's study of *The Radical Reformation* (Weidenfield and Nicolson, 1961), dealing with the broader context in which modern Unitarianism first arose.

These works have not yet been surpassed as the basic texts for the study of Unitarian history, but they are now rarely available without recourse to academic libraries. Williams's work, with its broader market, is still available in a paperback edition. Wilbur is now out of print, except for *Our Unitarian Heritage*, which can be accessed free of charge on the Internet at **http://www.sksm.edu/research/publications/ouh.pdf**.

Useful bibliographies, articles and obituaries will also be found on the website of the Unitarian Historical Society in Great Britain at **http://www.unitariansocieties.org.uk/historical/hsindex.html**. World Wide Web users will also find a mine of information in the online *Dictionary of Unitarian Universalist Biography* at **www.uua.org/uuhs/duub/**, an ongoing project of the American Unitarian Universalist Historical Society.

Charles Howe, *For Faith and Freedom: A Short History of Unitarianism in Europe* (Skinner House, 1997), was written as an epitome of Wilbur's two-volume *History of Unitarianism*, with material added from Williams's *Radical Reformation*. There is, consequently, an emphasis on the Reformation, leaving space for only brief treatment of Unitarianism in Great Britain.

Readers who want to go beyond the secondary accounts of Unitarian history and engage with the primary sources, which is to be encouraged, will find a range of extracts from Europe, Britain and America in David B. Parke, *The Epic of Unitarianism* (Beacon Press, 1957; Skinner House, 1985), interspersed with helpful commentaries.

The contentious relationship of British Unitarianism to early developments on the European continent is dealt with in G. Bonet-Maury, *Early Sources of English Unitarian Christianity* (British and Foreign Unitarian Association, 1884). Robert Wallace's now extremely rare *Antitrinitarian Biography* (E. T. Whitfield, 1850) is a mine of information about Unitarian pioneers on the continent, as well as in Great Britain.

Servetus is the subject of R. H. Bainton, *Hunted Heretic: The Life and Death of Michael Servetus* (Beacon Press, 1953; Blackstone Editions, 2005), and Marian Hillar, *Michael Servetus: Intellectual Giant, Humanist, and Martyr* (University Press of America, 2002). There is a biographical study of Castellio in R. H. Bainton, *The Travail of Religious Liberty* (Westminster Press, 1951).

An important primary source for the history of Socinianism and the Minor Reformed Church of Poland is Stanislas Lubienieki, *History of the Polish Reformation and Nine Related Documents*, translated and with commentaries by George Huntston Williams (Fortress Press, Minneapolis, 1995). It also provides contemporary information about early Unitarianism in Transylvania and the Italian radical reformers. Also useful for developments in Poland is Stanislas Kot, *Socinianism in Poland: The Social and Political Ideas of the Polish Antitrinitarians in the Sixteenth and Seventeenth Centuries* [trans. E. M. Wilbur] (Starr King Press, 1957). For the community at Raków see Phillip Hewett, *Racovia* (Blackstone Editions, 2004).

János Erdő provided a chronology of developments in Transylvania in his *Transylvanian Unitarian Church: Chronological History and Theological Essays* (Center for Free Religion, Chico, CA, 1990), but Dénes Lőrinczy, "The Hungarian Unitarian Church" in *Transactions of the Unitarian Historical Society*, 1923-26, written while he was the first Sharpe Scholar at Unitarian College Manchester, is still considered the best work in English.

The posthumously published doctoral thesis of Imre Gellérd, *A History of Transylvanian Unitarianism through Four Centuries of Sermons* (Uniquest, Chico, CA, 1999) is a survey of preaching in Transylvania.

A general treatment of Transylvanian history, in English, is István Lázár, *Transylvania: A Short History* (Corvina, Budapest, 1997), while the context of the changes that took place in Romania in December 1989 is movingly described in Laslo Tokes, *With God, for the People* (Hodder and Stoughton, 1990). Tokes was the Reformed pastor, now bishop of Nagyvarad, whose protest at Temesvar subsequently led to the uprising in Bucharest and the downfall of the Ceausescu regime. For Transylvania post-1989, I have relied primarily on Judit Gellerd's introduction to her father's published thesis, her own *Prisoner of Liberte: The Story of a Transylvanian Martyr* (Uniquest, 2003) and Mózes Kedei (ed.), *Confessions about Ourselves* (Transylvanian Ministers Fellowship, n.d.). I also owe much to conversations with Sharpe Scholars at Unitarian College between 1991 and 2002, but they have also left me without any real confidence that this period is yet being satisfactorily evaluated, either in Romania or abroad.

Sandor Kovacs, "Transylvania and Unitarian College, Manchester" in Leonard Smith (ed.) *Unitarian to the Core: Unitarian College, Manchester 1854-2004* (Carnegie Publishing, 2004) explains the special relationship the Transylvanian Church has maintained with British Unitarians for the further theological education of its ministers.

The Catechism of the Transylvanian Unitarian Church is on the Internet at **http://www.unitarius.hu/english/catechism.html**.

The situation in metropolitan Hungary is dealt with, in particular, by Bishop Joseph Ferencz, Jr., in *Hungarian Unitarianism in the Nineteenth and Twentieth Centuries* (The Center for Free Religion, Chico, CA, 1990).

For the Czech Unitarians, see Richard Henry, *Norbert Fabian Čapek: A Spiritual Journey* (Skinner House, 1999).

Sources for British Unitarianism are more numerous, though many are long since out of print. Alexander Gordon's *Heads of English Unitarian History* (British and Foreign Unitarian Association, 1895; facsimile edition, Cedric Chivers, Bath, 1970) provides a summary to the end of the nineteenth century. Two concise articles by R. K. Webb are commendable for their clarity and literary merit: "The Unitarian Background" in Barbara Smith (ed.), *Truth, Liberty, Religion: Essays celebrating Two Hundred Years of Manchester College* (Manchester College Oxford, 1986), and "English Unitarianism in the Nineteenth Century" in Leonard Smith (ed.), *Unitarian to the Core: Unitarian College Manchester, 1854-2004* (Carnegie Publishing, 2004).

Two primary sources have recently become available: Thomas Belsham, *Memoirs of Theophilus Lindsey MA* (Lensden CD ROM, 2007) and G. M. Ditchfield (ed.), *The Letters of Theophilus Lindsey (1723-1808): Vol. 1, 1747-1788* (The Boydell Press. 2007).

For Protestant Dissent generally, Michael R. Watts, *The Dissenters: Vol. 1, From the Reformation to the French Revolution* (Clarendon Press, 1978) is useful, and, to a lesser extent, so is *Vol. 2, The Expansion of Evangelical Nonconformity 1791-1859* (Clarendon Press, 1995).

More specifically, the origins of English Unitarianism in Old Dissent are dealt with in *The English Presbyterians: From Elizabethan Puritanism to Modern Unitarianism* (G. Allen & Unwin, 1968), a collection of chapters by C. G. Bolam, Jeremy Goring, H. L. Short and Roger Thomas, which unfortunately is destined forever to be wrongly catalogued as a work on Presbyterianism, rather than Unitarianism. The history of the dissenting academies, where Arian and Unitarian views emerged, is dealt with by H. J. McLachlan in *English Education Under the Test Acts* (Manchester University Press, 1931).

James Martineau's life, work and thought are extensively covered in James Drummond and C. B. Upton, *Life and Letters of James Martineau* (James Nisbet, 1902); C. B. Upton, *Martineau's Philosophy* (James Nisbet, 1905); J. Estlin Carpenter, *James Martineau* (Philip Green, 1905); and more recently by Ralph Waller in "James Martineau: The Development of his Religious Thought" in Barbara Smith (ed.) *Truth, Liberty, Religion* (Manchester College Oxford, 1986) and by Frank Schulman, *James Martineau: This Conscience-Intoxicated Unitarian* (Meadville Lombard Theological School Press, 2002). A short anthology, *James Martineau: Selections*, edited by Alfred Hall (Lindsey Press, 1950) makes palatable works that in their entirety are daunting. *A James Martineau Miscellany* (The Martineau Society, Oxford, 2005), edited by Sophia Hankinson, is a selection of recent lectures and articles by those working in this field, and a new biography by Ralph Waller is anticipated.

The particularities of Unitarianism in Wales are dealt with by D. Elwyn Davies in *They Thought for Themselves* (Gomer Press, 1982), and in Scotland by L. Baker Short in *Pioneers of Scottish Unitarianism* (H. G. Walters, 1963). Nineteenth-century British outgrowth to Canada is dealt with in Phillip Hewett, *Unitarians in Canada, 1810-1975* (Fitzhenry & Whiteside, 1978; second edition, Canadian Unitarian Council, 1995).

For Unitarian tendencies within Anglicanism, J. P. Ferguson, *Dr. Samuel Clarke: An Eighteenth Century Heretic* (Roundwood Press, 1976), deals with the Trinitarian Controversy and issues of Prayer Book revision.

Alexander Gordon, *Addresses Biographical and Historical* (Lindsey Press, 1922) contains studies of Servetus, Thomas Firmin, Theophilus Lindsey, Thomas Belsham and Richard Wright, and an account of the Salters' Hall Controversy.

A recent study of the threat to Unitarian property from orthodox Dissent in the nineteenth century is Frank Schulman, *Blasphemous and Wicked: The Unitarian Struggle for Equality 1813-1844* (Harris Manchester College Oxford, 1997).

There are two works dealing with Unitarianism's mid-nineteenth century accessions, both by H. J. McLachlan: *The Methodist Unitarians* (Manchester University Press, 1919) and *A Nonconformist Library* (Manchester University Press, 1923), which contains an article on "The Christian Brethren Movement." The General Baptists await an historian, though they are now receiving more attention from Baptist scholars and it still remains for someone to provide their history from a Unitarian viewpoint.

A summary of Unitarian social and political history is R. V. Holt, *The Unitarian Contribution to Social Progress in England* (G. Allen & Unwin, 1938), though the absence of references is disappointing. An entertaining description of the National Conference and General Assembly meetings between 1920 and 1945, reported in the style of Samuel Pepys, is R. P. Jones's *It Is Very Observable* (Lindsey Press, 1946).

The byways of the history of Unitarianism in Great Britain are explored in the numerous articles published in *Transactions of the Unitarian Historical Society,* 1917 to the present.

For part three, an additional major source was G. W. Cooke, *Unitarianism in America* (American Unitarian Association, Boston, 1902), which is profusely illustrated. More recently there has been Conrad Wright's *The Beginnings of Unitarianism in America* (Archon, 1966) and a work edited by him, *Stream of Light: A Sesquicentennial History of American Unitarianism* (Unitarian Universalist Association, Boston, 1975). H. H. Cheetham, *Unitarianism and Universalism* (Beacon Press, 1962) is a concise summary intended primarily for children's' religious education.

Conrad Wright, *The Unitarian Controversy* (Skinner House, 1994) and Conrad Edick Wright (ed.), *American Unitarianism, 1805-1865* (Massachusetts Historical Society, 1989) cover the major external and internal controversies of the nineteenth century.

Conrad Wright (ed.), *Three Prophets of Religious Liberalism: Channing, Emerson, Parker* (Beacon Press, 1961) makes available the three primary sources for this period, with an explanatory essay. These can also be found on the World Wide Web: Channing's Baltimore Sermon at **http://xroads.virginia.edu/%7EHYPER/DETOC/religion/unitarian. html**; Emerson's Divinity School Address at **http://www.emersoncentral. com/divaddr.htm**; and Parker's "The Transient and Permanent in Christianity" at **http://www.vcu.edu/engweb/transcendentalism/authors/ parker/transient.html** .

Two biographies of the life of Theodore Parker are Henry Steele Commager, *Theodore Parker: Yankee Crusader* (Beacon Press, 1960) and Dean Grodzins, *American Heretic: Theodore Parker and Transcendentalism* (University of North Carolina Press, 2002).

David Robinson, *The Unitarians and the Universalists* (Greenwood Press, 1985) is especially useful for its treatment of Transcendentalism. The best book on the history of Unitarianism in the Midwestern and Western states is Charles H. Lyttle, *Freedom Moves West* (Beacon Press, 1952; Blackstone Editions, 2006). For its chapter on "Henry W. Bellows and the Organization of the National Conference" see Conrad Wright, *The Liberal Christians* (Beacon Press, 1970).

John Allen Macaulay's *Unitarianism in the Antebellum South: The Other Invisible Institution* (University of Alabama Press, 1964) and J. D. Bowers's *Joseph Priestley and English Unitarianism in America* (Pennsylvania State University Press, 2007) give greater place to the influence of immigrant influences on the shaping of American Unitarianism, than the traditional New England interpretations have generally allowed.

For American Universalism, Ernest Cassara's *Universalism in America: A Documentary History* (Beacon Press, 1971) complements David Parke's *Epic of Unitarianism* in providing Universalism's primary sources. The major study of the movement is Russell E. Miller, *The Larger Hope*: *Vol. 1, The First Century of the Universalist Church in America 1770-1870* and *Vol. 2, The Second Century of the Universalist Church in America 1870-1970* (Unitarian Universalist Association, 1986). This monumental work is drawn upon by Charles Howe, *The Larger Faith: A Short History of American Universalism* (Skinner House, 1993), to provide a more concise account of the Universalists and a good explanation of the negotiations leading to the consolidation of the Universalist Church of America in the Unitarian Universalist Association. Other works are George Huntston Williams, *American Universalism: A Bicentennial Historical Essay* (1971; Skinner House, 1983, 2002) and Peter Hughes, "The Origins of New England Universalism: Religion without a Founder" in *The Journal of Unitarian Universalist History* (1997).

A relatively recent compendium by Mark W. Harris, *A Historical Dictionary of Unitarian Universalism* (Scarecrow Press, 2004), is particularly useful for its coverage of worldwide Unitarian movements. The major work on Unitarianism in India is Spencer Lavan, *Unitarians and India* (Skinner House, 1977). Additional information on worldwide Unitarianism can be found on the web site of the International Council of Unitarians and Universalists, **www.icuu.net/** and on the churches' own web sites linked to the ICUU site.

Glossary

Adventist - Anticipating the second coming of Christ.

Anabaptist (literally re-baptism) - A term used for those who rejected infant baptism in favor of adult, believer's baptism.

Antinomian - The views of those who believe that if a Christian is saved by grace and not by works or moral effort, then the saved are free from all moral obligations.

Arianism - The term originates with Arius, a priest of Alexandria, who in early Church controversies contended that God the Father was supreme and Christ subordinate, over against Athanasius who argued that the persons of the Trinity were coequal. The issue was settled at the Council of Nicaea in 325AD, when Arian opinion was judged heretical and Trinitarian Christianity became the orthodoxy. The term again came into use in the eighteenth century to describe those who while holding that Jesus as subordinate, still regarded him as semi-divine.

Arminian - The belief that human beings can be saved by making a personal response to Divine grace, in contrast to Calvinism which asserts that some (the elect) are predestined for salvation, some to be damned.

Atonement - The process by which the broken relationship between God and humankind is restored. Christian orthodoxy generally holds that by his death on the cross Jesus paid a debt to satisfy God for the disobedience of Adam. There were, even within orthodoxy, always other theories which maintained the breach could be healed by an ethical response to the death of Jesus (for example Peter Abelard). It was the "satisfactionary" theory that early radical anti-Trinitarians objected to as morally abhorrent.

Determinism - The philosophical thesis that any event whatsoever is an instance of some law of nature.

Evangelical - A term used to describe religion that asserts the centrality of Biblical revelation, the sinfulness of human nature and the necessity of personal salvation. (Not to be confused with Evangelism, which means spreading the faith.)

Evangelical Dissent - The term for the nonconformist traditions that were products of the eighteenth-century Evangelical Revival, and for the old dissenting bodies that were influenced by it, for example the Independents (Congregationalists) and Baptists.

Evangelical Revival - The religious phenomenon in eighteenth-century Britain which gave birth to Methodism, stemming from the conversion of John Wesley in 1738.

Gothic Revival - The adoption of gothic styles of architecture in the nineteenth century, which replaced the Classical styles of the eighteenth century. It was an aspect of the Romantic Movement.

Great Awakening - A spiritual phenomenon which occurred in New England in 1734, similar to the Evangelical Revival in Great Britain.

Great Ejection - The name given to the expulsion of Anglican clergy who refused to conform to the Act of Uniformity in 1662.

Lord's Supper - The term used by Protestants for the Communion Service.

Lutheran - Forms of Protestantism where the overriding influence was that of Martin Luther.

Materialism - The philosophy that everything is wholly dependent on matter for its existence and, more specifically, that there is only one fundamental kind of reality and this is material, and that human beings and other living creatures are not dual beings composed of a material body and an immaterial soul, but are fundamentally bodily in nature.

Necessarianism - Similar to Determinism, the thesis that actions are determined by prior history.

Occasional Conformity - The nonconformist custom of taking the sacrament periodically in the parish church, say once a year, to qualify for holding a public office, or a commission in the services.

Radical Reformation - A term used to designate the forms the Reformation took under the influence of reformers more radical than Martin Luther, John Calvin and Ulrich Zwingli.

Rational Dissent - Those nonconformist traditions, particularly the English Presbyterians and Unitarians, who held that religion was primarily to be determined by reason.

Reformed - The Protestant tradition that derived from the influence of John Calvin. Helvetic is occasionally used as an alternative, because it stemmed from Geneva, Switzerland.

Sabellianism - After Sabellius, a third or fourth-century theologian, who argued that God is one individual being and the terms Father, Son and Holy Spirit are simply names applied to the different forms (or modes) of action of the one being, which do not refer to eternal and intrinsic distinctions within the godhead. Modalism is an alternative name for Sabellianism.

Socinian - Literally it means relating to the doctrinal system of Faustus Socinus, but the term was very loosely used, and often as one of abuse for anyone whose opinions approached Unitarianism.

Test and Corporation Acts - The British Parliamentary measures that prevented Dissenters from holding public office, until they were repealed in 1828.

Transcendentalism - A school of religious thought, philosophy and literature that developed in America in the nineteenth century, which asserted that religion was essentially a matter of emotion and feeling, rather than to be determined intellectually. The term derives from the opinion of the Transcendentalists (Emerson, Thoreau, et al.) that their religion transcended codification.

Universalism - In contrast to Calvinism, where salvation was limited to the elect, and to Arminianism, where it was limited to those who made a specific response to the grace of God offered in Jesus Christ, Universalism was the belief that all would ultimately be saved. A more recent development has been the tendency to use the term to describe forms of religious practice that draw on World Faiths.

Index